P9-DCQ-719

TRANSPORTATION

IN

THE WORLD

OF

THE FUTURE

TRANSP

ORTATION
IN
THE WORLD
OF
THE FUTURE

NEW, REVISED EDITION

BY

HAL HELLMAN

WITHDRAWN
From
Poynter Jr. High Library

M. Evans and Company, Inc.
NEW YORK, N.Y. 10017

J. W. Poynter Jr. H. S. Library
1535 N. E. Grant St.
Hillsboro, Oregon 97123

IN MEMORY OF

Julius Robley Almer

ACKNOWLEDGMENTS

The list of people who have contributed time, information or material
to this book is a long one, and the author regrets that it is not possible
to thank all of them here. He would, however, like to acknowledge the
assistance provided by the following: Prof. J. V. Foa of Rensselaer Polytechnic Institute, Mr. Bruce J. Firkins of General Electric, Prof. R. J.
Hanson of M.I.T., Mr. Leon Katz of the Port of New York Authority,
and Mr. Myron Miller, who at the time the first edition of this book
was being prepared, was Senior Engineer at the U.S. Department of
Transportation's Office of High Speed Ground Transportation. Mr. Miller
provided much useful information and was kind enough to review the
manuscript as well. His comments were very useful. For the revised
edition a similar role was played by Mr. Edward J. Ward, who is Chief,
Advanced Systems Division, of DOT's Office of Research, Development
and Demonstration. I am deeply indebted to both men.

H. H.

M. Evans and Company titles are distributed in
the United States by the J. B. Lippincott Company,
East Washington Square, Philadelphia, Pa. 19105,
and in Canada by McClelland & Stewart Ltd.
25 Hollinger Road, Toronto M4B, 3G2, Ontario.

WITHDRAWN
From
Pointer Jr. High Library
7669

Copyright © 1968, 1974 by Hal Hellman
All rights reserved under International and
Pan American Copyright Conventions
Library of Congress Catalog Card Number: 73-68220
ISBN 0–87131–155–0
Manufactured in the United States of America

9 8 7 6 5 4 3 2 1

Contents

*Other books by Hal Hellman
in the World of the Future series:*

BIOLOGY IN THE WORLD OF THE FUTURE
THE CITY IN THE WORLD OF THE FUTURE
COMMUNICATIONS IN THE WORLD OF THE FUTURE
ENERGY IN THE WORLD OF THE FUTURE
FEEDING THE WORLD OF THE FUTURE

Prologue

ON HIS WAY into the kitchen, Andrew Mann touched the "Car" button on the electronic communications panel in the living room. By the time he had finished breakfast a rented Electra-car, delivered automatically from the town depot, was waiting for him at the door.

Andrew slid into the sleek two-seater, inserted his All-Credit card (which acted as both ignition key and accounting agent), stepped on the accelerator, and was on his way.

A short two-mile drive brought him to the electronic highway. As he approached the entrance, he punched out his destination on the dashboard console, which automatically beamed the information, plus the car code, to the highway control computer.

Immediately, the computer announced via his car radio, "Sorry, Mr. Mann, but you will have to wait about two minutes before you can get onto the Autoway. We have just reached critical density. However, if you will drive onto the ramp at your right, you can relinquish manual control; the automatic system will take over and will check out your car at the same time.

"I see," continued Highway Control, "that you are going to the Long Distance Transportation Terminal in New York. Since traffic is particularly heavy this morning, some of the vehicles are being routed through the new Hudson Tunnel. Your distance to the terminal is therefore 28 miles; the trip will take 17 minutes. I will inform you when you are approaching your destination. Please switch to automatic now."

Andrew Mann flicked the proper switch and relaxed. "Now for an important decision," he chuckled. "Shall I read, sleep, or watch the news . . . ?"

Andrew opened his eyes. He could feel the car decelerating smoothly but perceptibly. His car radio came on and a gentle voice said, "Mr. Mann, you are approaching the terminal. We hope you enjoyed your ride. Thank you."

Andrew shook himself slightly and mumbled, "So soon?" He checked his cathode ray tube map display. Sure enough, the little white dot showed that he was entering the midtown New York area. "Hm. Must have slept right through the ride."

The Electra-car, still moving at a rapid clip, entered the new Hudson Tunnel and a moment later came to a smooth halt in the basement of the giant Long Distance Treminal. Andrew got out, punched the "Park" button, and watched the car glide off—to be used by someone else. He mused, "Seems to me I read somewhere that people had to park their own cars a hundred years ago. Seems hard to believe."

A few steps brought him to the glidewalk. He stepped on and a female voice sounded in his ear: "Welcome, traveler, to the first fully integrated public transportation system on earth. Where are you bound?"

"Area 303, Oakland, California."

"Oh, I'm sorry, but the hypersonic transport has just left, and there won't be another one for two hours."

"That's all right. I'm in no rush and I would like to try the 'Tube' anyway. I've never used it before."

"Fine. The next train comes through from Boston in twenty-five minutes. A pod is waiting, however, in the subterminal. I suggest you get off the glidewalk at Exit Two, which you will reach in a few moments. You will see the pod to the right of the Exit sign. How much luggage do you have with you?"

"Just a hand case. I can handle it."

"Good. Do you have your All-Credit card with you?"

"Yes."

"Would you please show it to the accounting machine on your right?"

Andrew flashed his card, and the computer's voice continued, "Thank you. We'll charge your travel account at the end of the month. Will that be satisfactory?"

"Yes, that's fine."

"As you probably know, the main train does not stop as it comes through. The pod will be accelerated to the same speed as the main section and will then hook onto it. The train travels at roughly 1,000 mph. Therefore, your trip will take just under three hours, and will bring you into the San Francisco terminal at 0917 local time."

Andrew grinned and glanced at his watch. It read 0925.

"At the terminal," his guide continued, "you have a choice of transportation modes. Are you perhaps going to the new two-mile-high building in Oakland?"

"Why, yes. I am."

"Well, in that case you could use the new Ele-car, which would take you directly from the terminal to the building and then up to the floor of your choice. Or, since you are not in a great hurry and might like to get up above ground for a while, we would suggest that you take the Air-Cushion Vehicle. It leaves directly from the terminal, crosses the bay, and continues right into Oakland. It's a beautiful ride. The ACV then connects with a minibus that will take you to your destination. However, the total trip may be lengthened by ten minutes or so."

"That's all right. The air-cushion mode sounds like a good idea."

"Very well, then. When you get off at the San Francisco terminal, take the escalator marked 'ACV.' Incidentally, don't worry about the details. You will receive printed instructions on the train. All right, step off here, please."

Andrew stepped off sideways onto a belt that was moving in the same direction as he was, but more slowly, and then finally onto solid ground. He walked toward the pod, a sleek silver train-car—without windows.

His unseen companion anticipated his question. "Although there are no windows in the train, a large Three-D screen will show highlights of the areas through which you will be passing on your cross-country trip. There are also small screens and earpieces which will provide a wide choice of private entertainment; they may be used for long-distance calls, if you wish. For your further convenience, an auto-barber, a snack bar, and a dictatyper are also available. If you need anything else, please ring. There is a hostess on board who will be happy to serve you. Goodbye now."

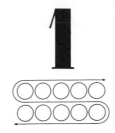

Today's World
of Transportation

THAT WAS quite a vision, wasn't it? Oddly enough, while a great deal of what went on during Mr. Mann's trip sounds very "far-out," none of it is impossible. There is nothing which controverts the laws of nature (as we know them today), such as anti-gravity or movement through time.

You may not believe this, but of all the items mentioned the one that will be most difficult to achieve will be the one that you probably didn't pay any attention to at all. I refer to the phrase used by Mr. Mann's guide and "companion," namely ". . . the first fully integrated public transportation system on earth."

Today, a person taking a trip may have to contend with
auto traffic, a bus system, a subway system, a train system,
an airline, and perhaps even a ship or ferry. Rarely do the
employees of one of these systems have any idea of what
the other systems are doing by way of schedules or prices,
and still less often do they care. What information they do
have stems more from feelings of competition than of cooperation or aid to the passenger.

One disgusted traveler put it this way: "We in the United
States have the greatest transportation system in the world
today. The only people who disagree are those who have
tried to use it."

In truth, we do not have a transportation system. We have
many. Sometimes they meet. Sometimes they almost meet.
And sometimes they are on opposite sides of a city.

So there are two parts to the problem. One is the actual
movement of people and goods. The other is the transfer
process from one system to another. Transferees can expect little help in the process. Most travelers from city to
city, or even from one section of a city to another, find they
are quite on their own. Many a weary and bewildered traveler (not to mention daily commuter) would be thankful to
have even a small part of our dream come true.

Can it? This is one of the questions we will explore in this
book. Another question is: How far are we from that mil-
lennium? A third is concerned with what is being done now
which will (or may) make that dream come true.

Transportation and the City

Before we go into these questions more carefully, we
should look at the world of transportation, including city
transportation, as it exists today. We start off with a fact that

may surprise you, as it did me. The average American family spends about 14 per cent of its income on transportation—for work, education, recreation, and social purposes. In some cities, such as Los Angeles and Detroit, the figure is more like 18 per cent. And as a nation, when we include industry, the proportion rises to a full 20 per cent, one-fifth of our Gross National Product. That's $200 billion just to move ourselves and our goods.

About half the amount spent goes into the movement of goods. Indeed, the average city dweller consumes some 18 tons of material annually. Every bit of it must be brought in from the outside. For, in contrast to farm and forest dwellers, city people cannot supply themselves with food, clothing, and shelter.

There are some who say that the city is doomed, that improvements in communications and transportation make it less necessary to concentrate in small areas than before. They say, furthermore, that increasing congestion is making it harder for commerce and industry to operate in crowded downtown areas, causing these businesses to flee to the suburbs. New York is cited as a prime example.

Yet, since World War II, more new office space has been built in New York City than exists in any other city in the world. One can hardly call this dying. What has happened, however, is more clearly seen in the residential areas of cities. These are indeed either losing population or barely holding their own, while the surrounding areas—the suburbs —are truly exploding.

Is this coincidence? Did it just happen to happen now? No, the forces at work in city and suburb have been strongly influenced by developments in transportation. In other words, transportation is not merely a set of devices or a means for moving vehicles from one place to another. It is a basic force in shaping the course of our lives. Indeed, the history of civilization might be described as the history of transportation.

For centuries, until the early 1800's, travel was limited to foot and horse. The worker, and his boss, therefore, were both limited to living no more than about two or three miles —a comfortable commuting distance—from the center of a city where most employment took place. Hence cities were quite limited in size, normally covering no more than about twenty square miles, but contained a highly dense population.

As recently as a century ago, one could see streams of walkers two and three miles long converging on the central area of London. In the 1890's, a thousand horse-buses were carrying over 100 million passengers per year into that city.

But change was in the air. Development in the late 1800's of the streetcar (or trolley), the railroad and rapid transit system (for example, the subway and "elevated") expanded the radius of urban movement to about five miles; the urban area (city plus suburbs) then covered perhaps eighty square miles.

The working-class suburbs of Chicago, Boston, and Philadelphia were literally created around the turn of the century by the newly built street-railway systems which radiated out from the city centers. In 1900 the most densely populated residential area of Manhattan, the East Side, contained almost 500,000 people in its most crowded square mile; today, due largely to the development of the city's rapid transit system, no square mile in the area now has more than 200,000 residents. In other words, the improved transport systems allowed increasing numbers of workers to live outside of the Central Business District (CBD) where most of them worked.

With the development of the automobile, the commuting radius expanded to 25 miles and even further. Urban areas now cover upwards of 2,000 square miles—one hundred times larger than the largest city of former times. Unfortunately, the poor cannot afford autos; they are pretty well restricted to living in or very close to the city centers.

The Modern Megalopolis

The expansion continues. Each year, urban America spreads at the rate of a million acres—an area as large as the state of Rhode Island. Today over two-thirds of all Americans live in one of the great metropolitan areas such as New York, Chicago, or Los Angeles. By 1980 more than three out of every four Americans will be living in and around such cities. By the end of this century the figure may be as high as 90 per cent.

Indeed, by 1980 the metropolitan areas will have expanded so greatly that some of the larger metropolises will begin to meet and merge into what has been named a *megalopolis*. (This word is from the Greek and means "great city." There actually was a city called Megalopolis in ancient Greece!)

By the year 2000, says urban expert Jerome P. Pickard, more than half of all Americans will be crammed into just two such areas. More than two-fifths will live in a single such region. Dubbed the Metropolitan Belt, this region, he says, will stretch from Maine to Virginia on the east and then westward to Illinois and Wisconsin (see map). Another 13 per cent of the population will live in what Pickard calls the California Urban Region, and five per cent will be concentrated in the Florida Peninsula Urban Region.

The large-scale concentration of people and resources in metropolitan areas has been made possible by improved transportation. The Regional Plan Association of New York

TRANSPORTATION
IN THE WORLD OF THE FUTURE

By the year 2000, over half of all Americans may live in these 3 urban regions.

Metropolitan Belt = 40% of the people
California Urban Region = 13% of the people
Florida Peninsula Urban Region = 5% of the people

estimates that, every weekday, 40 million one-way trips are made in this area, and over three million commuters enter the nine-square-mile section of Manhattan south of 61st Street. It seems clear that the economic, social, and cultural opportunities of urban living are being sought by more and more people.

But, says transportation expert Wilfred Owen, metropolitan cities have now grown to the point where they threaten to strangle the transportation that made them possible. A new "law" of transportation says: The longer the distance, the shorter the time needed to cover it. And indeed, it does often take longer to drive from the heart of Manhattan to La Guardia Airport—a distance of about seven miles—than it does to fly from La Guardia to Boston (220 miles) or even Detroit (650 miles).

Congestion in and above airports is another problem, with aircraft sometimes having to wait an hour or more just to take off or land. The FAA (Federal Aviation Administration) says that it takes a person the same length of time (eight hours) to get from his home in Chicago to downtown Los Angeles as it took ten years ago. Thus, increases in ground and air congestion have completely cancelled reductions in flight time resulting from improved flight routings and faster aircraft.

Today's Staggering Problems— and Some Suggested Answers

Every city in the United States is faced with a transportation problem of staggering proportions, one which will undoubtedly get worse before it gets better. Many other areas of the world, where population is still growing at an explosive pace, will eventually face similar problems.

Two other factors that serve to increase the amount of passenger and freight movement are the continually larger areas being served by central cities, and higher incomes (at least in the more highly developed nations). As people move up the economic ladder, increased expenditure for transportation always follows.

At the same time, passengers have shifted increasingly from rail to road, putting gigantic strains on already antiquated and overburdened street systems. About half of all CBD (Central Business District) land is occupied by streets, sidewalks, and parking facilities. In areas that depend heavily on cars for transportation, such as Los Angeles, the figure rises to almost two-thirds of all CBD land—just for streets and parking!

There is also the matter of safety. Every year in the United States alone, 55,000 people are killed and three million more are injured in automobile accidents. This far exceeds all other modes of transport combined, even when the higher proportion of auto travel is considered. Clearly, something must be done about this.

We see then that the problems are varied. We already mentioned the plight of the traveler who must switch from one system to another. An additional, and major, problem is the pendulum swing of commuters during the peak morning and evening "rush" hours. The tempers, time, and energy lost, and the air pollution produced, are beyond belief. The "speed" of traffic during these periods frequently falls to a few miles an hour, and sometimes to zero.

Subways, of course, do not have this problem. But while they do a fantastic job of moving great numbers of people in reasonable time, they are often more fit for sardines than humans during rush hours. Yet in the off hours they attract relatively few customers. The problem here, therefore, is how to provide satisfactory capacity during rush hours without having a lot of equipment and men doing nothing for the rest of the day, and particularly at night.

Another transportation problem is providing for weekend and holiday travel. There isn't one of us living in or near a metropolitan area who hasn't battled—and lost to—ten to 15 miles of creeping cars.

But what is simply inconvenience for us is "death" to certain types of businesses, particularly manufacturing and shipping. With improved roads and highways outside the cities, it has been possible for many of them to move away from the CBD, to spread out into the suburbs. But this is exactly where the poor and unskilled, who provide most of the labor market for industries, cannot live. The poor depend upon mass transit. However, population density in the suburbs is too low to support rail systems. Buses help, but they are normally subject to traffic tie-ups no less than cars.

Thus, the poor are moving into the city centers in great numbers, while their employers—the larger manufacturers particularly—are moving out. On the other hand, the skilled and white-collar workers are moving farther and farther out, leading often to two-hour commuting trips each way.

The various problems we have mentioned thus far boil down to this: How to provide safe, fast, convenient, comfortable transportation for both urban and suburban dwellers.

One of the answers has been the 42,500-mile Interstate Highway System, the most enormous public works project the world has ever seen, surpassing by far the Pyramids and the Great Wall of China. When completed sometime in the late 1970's, the total cost is likely to be around $80 billion.

Although these highways have certainly made travel a pleasure in many ways and in many areas, not everyone agrees that they are the answer. It is pointed out, for example, that they encourage auto travel, and thereby serve to funnel even more traffic into the already overburdened cities. It has been estimated that if all New York commuters were to arrive by car, every bit of land in the CBD would be required for parking—with some cars left over. And, as we shall see later, in addition to being expensive, the roads themselves eat up land at a prodigious rate.

But what was a bad dream only a few years ago has turned into a nightmare; our gleaming automotive lines of transportation have become a net that threatens to strangle us. And what was once almost entirely a big-city problem is now also occurring in almost every medium-sized city, and in many small towns as well.

Nor is this the end of our tale of woe. Two additional problems have loomed large since the first edition of this book was published in 1968. One is an energy shortage. There is talk of gasoline rationing and there are actual shortages here and there of fuel oil, natural gas, and electricity. Automobiles, unfortunately, are a highly inefficient mode of transport in terms of fuel consumption.

Allied with this problem is air pollution. Although it was clear even in 1968 that air pollution was a serious health hazard, it was not even mentioned in this section, being reserved for the chapter on the city center.

Both these factors—energy supply and environmental considerations—have had a great impact on the political decisions that have been made in the interim, and have greatly strengthened the position of the proponents of public transportation. For the first time in the history of the United States, there is a cabinet-level Department of Transportation (DOT), providing hope that a national transportation program and system can be devised which will solve some of the major problems.

The DOT Act was passed on October 15, 1966. It is worth reprinting the first paragraph of the Act:

The Congress hereby declares that the general welfare, the economic growth and stability of the Nation and its security require the development of national transportation policies and programs conducive to the provision of fast, safe, efficient, and convenient transportation at the lowest cost consistent therewith and with other national objectives, including the efficient utilization and conservation of the Nation's resources.

An important aspect of Secretary's job is that he is concerned with transportation as a whole, rather than with protecting the interests of any particular transportation system or agency. Indeed, one of the major jobs of the Secretary has been to pull together 100,000 people in more than 30 different agencies that had traditionally dealt with air, rail, water, and highway transportation. This consolidation, plus the authority vested in DOT, should enable the Department to cope with many problems that were well beyond the scope of any earlier agencies, and to cope as well with the many interagency rivalries which still exist.

In addition, the Department has a powerful tool—*research,* One of the advantages of a large agency is the availability of funds with which to encourage and support large-scale research. This research is needed to provide varied answers to a many-sided problem.

For example, the fantastic spread of the car has dampened the public's earlier enthusiasm for rail transportation. Many commuter railroads are either bankrupt or on the way. Many have had to be taken over by state agencies. Service is slow, inconvenient, and getting worse.

The problem compounds itself. No system can afford to operate only during peak hours. So workers are laid off and equipment is retired. This impairs service further, and more riders are lost. One suburban line in New Jersey, once a thriving concern, now runs only three trains a day. A recent traffic study shows that 94 per cent of those who both live and work in the suburbs use cars for their commuting.

The issue in recent years has been trains *vs.* cars. Stated this way, there is no right answer. Rather, the question should be how best to utilize both systems, for both are needed. Here is where technology can come to the rescue.

Systems are being considered which may combine the best features of the two. The result might be an automatic expressway such as Andrew Mann used in our Prologue. Systems like this shall be our major concern in the following chapters.

Rail Rapid Transit

THE FIRST transit system in the United States was a "public stage." For a fee, it shuttled New Yorkers between Bowling Green, at the lower tip of Manhattan, and Bleecker Street, which was all of one and three-quarter miles to the north.

The stages—horse-drawn carriages—made their first runs in 1830. They were private enterprises that catered to a slowly growing middle class rather than to the poor, who could not afford such luxuries, or to the rich, who had their own horses and buggies.

A few years later, the first railroad lines began taking people out into the country. In the case of New York, this meant going all the way up to what is now mid-Manhattan for picnics and outings.

The next major development in transit travel came in the 1890's. Rising wages for skilled workers increased demand for transit, while at the same time low wages for laborers made transit facilities cheap to build. Suddenly, every American city, and many towns, sprouted shining new lines of trolley track. Trolleys, or streetcars, were more convenient for local travel than railroads, since they traveled on the local streets and could stop at every corner if necessary. Furthermore, they provided a far smoother ride than stages, which moved upon the lumpy, bumpy cobblestones or plain dirt that were the common surfaces then. The rails also made life much easier for the horses still pulling the stages!

Electrification of the trolley systems made them cleaner and more exciting. In the early 1900's, New York City alone had 683 miles of trolley track within the city limits. It was even possible to ride all the way up to Boston on trolley tracks, paying 48 five-cent fares along the way. The idea of the modern megalopolis may sound like a new one, but this aspect of the several-hundred-mile city was evident more than half a century ago.

But trolleys, having neither the speed advantage conferred by the railroad's exclusive right-of-way, nor the flexibility of the bus, lost out to both. Because no exclusive rights-of-way were involved, the disappearance of trolley lines caused no major dislocations. The tracks, most of which had been laid in existing streets, were simply taken out or covered over.

The railroads, on the other hand, continued to grow. Indeed, the nineteenth and early twentieth centuries saw the railroads grow to arrogant giants. So powerful, so confident were the managements of their monopoly position in the field of transportation that they ignored the threat of those two youngsters, the automobile and, not much later, the aircraft. There was little concern or planning for the future.

It turns out that the rails in railroading, once the basis for its strength, are now its curse. For the truth is that, in many areas, the rails simply do not run to the right places any more. They are not where the "action" is.

Central cities with a population of a million or more—
where the railroad is feasible (suitable for commuting, for
example)—saw some increased growth during the 1960's, but
not much. The number of such cities increased from five to
six. On the other hand, of the 25 largest cities, twelve actually lost population. Yet—a seeming contradiction—the total
population of the United States grew by 24 million during
that same period of time.

Where did all these people go? Mostly, to the suburbs.
Generally speaking, 80 per cent of the population growth of
the last decade took place in urban areas—cities plus their
suburbs. And 80 per cent of *this* growth took place in the
suburbs. For the first time in our history the number of persons living in suburban areas is greater than that inside the
cities.

Once, cities and towns had to be centered on railroad stations and depots; with the development of motor vehicle
and air transportation, this is no longer necessary.

But rights-of-way, once obtained, and rails, once laid, are
not easily transferred. The investment in existing rights-of-
way and rail lines is gigantic.

It is tempting to say, "If the railroads are not economically
sound and if people prefer cars, let the railroads go the way
of the horse and buggy. Let the laws of supply and demand
make the decision."

This would be shortsighted, and even unfair. What happens then to the young, the poor, the old, the infirm, or even
those who, for various reasons, prefer not to own cars? Let
us remember, too, the problem of congestion we have already mentioned.

A single rail line can carry far more passengers than a lane
of highway—depending on circumstances, from five to
twenty times as many. Since population is increasing in urban
areas, it may be that rail lines that are not profitable now may

again become so later on, especially with the help of some developments we shall discuss as we go along.

One of the major reasons for the unprofitability of public transit is labor costs. In some transit systems the labor costs alone amount to 110 per cent of the system's income. Yet, in comparing auto and train travel, the value of the driver's time is never counted. In New York State the transit deficit runs about $150 million a year. Nationwide the urban transit deficit in 1972 (not counting suburban railroads), was $513 million.

Automation is clearly a possible (and probably the only) way to make public transit pay for itself. Unfortunately, labor contracts in existing systems make it practically impossible to introduce automation. And, of course, there are the strictly technical difficulties of revamping a busy, ongoing business.

New systems are another matter, however, and we are seeing new and very hopeful ventures. In 1969 America's first automated transit line began operation. Lindenwold is a 14 1/2-mile commuter-type railroad connecting Philadelphia with several South New Jersey communities. There are no conductors on board. Only one man operates each train, and his only function is to open and close doors and to push a button which starts the train out of each station. The system controls the acceleration and deceleration of the train and does a much better job of it than a man could. Gone are the slight jerks that one usually feels as manually controlled trains move out of stations.

The stations, too, are unattended, though they are monitored by television from a central office. An automatic fare-collection service was designed to eliminate station cashiers and to make it unnecessary for any employee to handle money. Cars are quiet, comfortable, and on time. Both cars and stations are air-conditioned. The complete trip runs 22 minutes with all stops; the same trip by car averages a full hour.

Thanks to these advantages, ridership has climbed steadily, and is now up to 42,000 per day. A survey indicates that 40 per cent of the riders were formerly car commuters. Parking lots holding as many as 8,000 cars at outlying stations are normally filled to capacity.

But most important of all, the line has made a profit. In 1972, it collected almost $700,000 more in fares than it spent to operate the line.

While these expenses do not cover the cost of construction, which was absorbed by the parent Delaware River Port Authority, the ability of the line to operate in the black is nevertheless considered a major achievement. Thus far virtually every other commuter and rapid transit line in this country and abroad loses money. Further, the construction of every transit system from now on is expected to be heavily subsidized. In 1970 Congress passed the Urban Mass Transportation Assistance Act, which provides two-thirds of the cost of construction for rapid transit systems. There is also some movement to increase this percentage to 90 per cent and provide money for operating expenses as well.

Automation has been carried even a step further on the newer, and much larger, San Francisco Bay Area Rapid Transit (BART) system. In 1972, 28 miles of the eventual 75-mile system were opened. The photo on page 24 shows the handsome lines of one of the highly automated trains.

Thanks to fully automatic controls, the trains are capable of 90-second headways (a train every 90 seconds). Maximum speed is kept to 80 mph, although the trains are capable of higher speeds. No human brain could possibly react fast enough to handle reliably a series of trains moving that fast and close together. The control system—a combination of local and central control—dispatches the trains, keeps them on schedule, opens and closes the doors, starts and stops the

A BART train and the Central Control Room which monitors the whole system.

trains, and maintains the proper interval between them. As with the Lindenwold system, there is just one person aboard each train, but he goes along mainly for reassurance to the passengers—and also to be on hand in case of trouble. As with any new and complicated system, there have been problems in operation, but these are being worked out.

Urban Railroad Systems

Interest in public transport has burgeoned since the first edition of this book was published.

Not only are new systems being built, old ones are being rejuvenated as well. The Long Island Railroad is one of the nation's busiest commuter lines, carrying a quarter of a million passengers every working day. Long a money-loser, it was bought by New York State from its former parent, the Penn Central. The cost for the entire system, with its 320 miles of right-of-way, its equipment, management, and skilled work force, was $65 million. Dr. William C. Ronan, chairman of the New York Metropolitan Transportation Authority (MTA), points out:

> This sum wouldn't have built two miles of the Cross-Bronx Expressway. We think we got a pretty good deal. . . . The cost of alternate highways—26 lanes of expressways plus new tunnels—would be over a billion and a half dollars, and there would be no place to park the cars.

A modernization program is bringing to the line some very handsome equipment, including air-conditioned, carpeted, and walnut-paneled cars. On the other hand, I rode the line not too long ago and was stunned to find that every single window in the once beautiful new car I was riding in was cracked or broken! How does one deal with such senseless vandalism?

Experiments are in progress on cars which can use third-rail electric power where available, or their own turbine engines in non-electrified areas farther out. Commuter train systems across the country are watching this program with great interest, for electrification is an expensive process; yet the burning of fossil fuels within city limits, even for trains, is being increasingly frowned upon. In addition, both types

25

provide higher acceleration capability than the currently used diesels. The acceleration factor is an important one, for much time is lost getting the heavy trains back up to speed after each stop.

Accelerating a heavy object like a train also uses up great amounts of energy. This is particularly a problem on rapid transit systems within cities, where stops are frequent. Interestingly, large amounts of energy are also required to stop the trains, which goes off as heat. The MTA is evaluating a system, called an onboard energy pack, on two New York City subway cars. Some form of energy storage system, in this case a large flywheel, is provided. The energy normally lost to heat when the train is brought to a stop is now delivered to the storage system, and it is then made available when needed to help the train get moving again. It is expected that 20 to 50 per cent of the propulsion energy will be conserved; also heat production will be cut, which will be a great boon in subway tunnels on hot summer days. And, finally, the train is assured of having enough power to move to the next station in the event of a power blackout.

A different approach to the acceleration-deceleration problem was taken on the Montreal Metro, which opened in 1966. Each station was built at the top of a slight grade; thus the train is helped by gravity to slow down when it arrives at a station, and to accelerate as it departs.

Another interesting aspect of the Montreal system is that it uses rubber tires! Eight big tires on each car ride on precast concrete runways, providing a smooth, silent ride. The system is cleaner too, for the rubber tires do not generate the dust that steel wheels on steel rail do. A special, nightly vacuum-train picks up whatever dust does arise.

The trains are guided by small, horizontal, rubber wheels which press against vertical rails. As a safety measure, the designers added a set of steel wheels which ride above steel rails and only contact them if tires should go flat. The steel wheels are also used for switching purposes, which would be a problem with rubber tires.

A large number of rail rapid transit systems are being built or considered in cities throughout the United States and the world. Some, such as the already built Mexico City and Montreal systems, are very beautiful, with architectural elegance and decoration. Others, like the New York City system, are chambers of horror. But all share one characteristic. They are efficient. During peak hours they may move as many as 60,000 people per hour per line. Automobile expressways can barely manage 1,500 or 2,000 cars per lane per hour. Figuring 1.5 passengers to a car—the true average is about 1.4—this adds up to only 3,000 passengers per lane per hour, or only one-twentieth the capacity of the rail line. It should also be noted that in large cities like New York and Chicago, 85 to 90 per cent of all commuters travel by public transit—rail and bus.

People Movers

But how about medium-density areas, where it is not economical to build, maintain, and run a complex, large-scale rail transit system? Where traffic is not heavy, the cost of manning and running the normal train or subway becomes prohibitive. Are such areas to be denied the acknowledged advantages of a rail system?

There is only one answer here, and that is a combination of smaller vehicles, protected guideways, and complete automation. Buses of course are smaller than trains; but without protected guideways, automated operation, at least at present, is out of the question.

A number of new systems have been designed and a few

have already been, or are being, built. The general term for them is People Movers. They are also sometimes called Personal Rapid Transit (PRT) systems, but for reasons that will become apparent later, I prefer the first name.

Two such systems are already being used in airports to provide rapid, convenient transportation between terminals, parking areas, hotels, etc. These, in today's giant airports, are often large distances apart. A Westinghouse system is operating at Tampa and an LTV system at the new Dallas/ Fort Worth airport. The latter, called Airtrans, has 13 miles of guideway; and the cars, which can operate singly or in combination, hold 40 persons—16 seated and 24 standing. Mail, luggage, and trash are also transported through the system, though special cars and in some cases special guideways are used.

Perhaps most exciting of all is a system under construction in Morgantown, West Virginia. Connecting three widely separated campuses of West Virginia University and the downtown section of Morgantown, its purpose is twofold: to serve the 20,000 WVU students, plus the faculty and staff, and the 29,000 inhabitants of Morgantown; and as a demonstration-research project for other small cities of the nation.

Initially, the Morgantown PRT is to have six stations, 3.2 miles of elevated track, and about one hundred vehicles, each of which can carry eight seated and seven standing passengers at speeds up to 30 miles an hour. The vehicles will operate in two modes—on a scheduled basis during busy times (class changes), and on a demand basis like elevators. Because the system is so new, costs are hard to figure; but it is hoped that students will be able to ride as many times as they wish for ten cents a day. Average time between stations is about two minutes.

It is interesting to note that while rapid transit systems in

A driverless "People Mover" on a test run in Morgantown, W. Va.

general have lost patronage, most of the loss has occurred in off-hour usage; peak-hour use has remained practically constant. Although the initial cost of an automated system is higher than an operator-controlled one, it will escape the problem of wage escalation that is plaguing all other non-automated systems. But perhaps more important, it will make available virtually instant service at all hours; this should go far to make People Movers economically viable. Two-way communications from each car to the central control office should help take away the feeling of being too much "on your own" in case of trouble.

Monorails

When speaking of modern rail technology, one almost always thinks of the monorail: sleek trains gracefully suspended from a single track. Yet, contrary to the usual notion, the first monorail was built more than a century ago. Still, while they are often seen at world fairs (e.g., at both the Seattle and New York World's Fairs) and on test tracks, they have found little commercial use.

One notable exception is the monorail at Wuppertal, West Germany, which has carried well over a billion passengers since 1900. In 1964, Tokyo built one linking its airport with the center of the city, a distance of 8.2 miles. And there is one in use at Disney World.

One of the advantages cited for use of the monorail is the fact that only a single rail need be put up for each line. With improved rail construction techniques, this advantage has faded somewhat. Also, monorail cars tend to sway and often require special horizontal wheels and tracks, thus negating the supposed simplicity of the system.

Perhaps some sort of compromise has been reached with General Electric's proposal for an Aerial Transport System. Based on a French system, the SAFEGE, it seems at first glance to be a monorail system; but it isn't, at least not in the normal sense of the world. The Aerial Transport System uses rubber wheels running on a pair of enclosed overhead tracks, and therefore offers quiet, smooth, and reliable operation under all weather conditions.

Clearly, it offers great advantages in low or medium density, cold-weather areas. Speeds of 100 mph are said to be quite feasible, even in ice and sleet, which normally make both air and surface travel slow and even hazardous. Again, completely automatic operation can make this a highly reliable and economical system. The latter factor becomes particularly marked when the Aerial Transport System is compared to subways, which are very expensive to build.

The illustration shows its possible usage as a direct connection between an airport (such as Dulles International, located about 25 miles from downtown Washington, D.C.) and the center of town.

The single-track arrangement shown might even be feasible right in or around the heart of a city, as a loop. That is, all trains would run in the same direction around a more or less circular track. The single track (or track pair) would take up less room than the normal two-way arrangement. Since CBD's are usually small, the passenger would not lose much time by having to travel, for example, three-quarters of the way around the loop to get to his destination.

One big advantage of any monorail type system is the small amount of surface area it requires. It is a natural for operation in built-up, though not heavily congested, areas. Supporting columns can be set in the center parkway of a street, if available, or just back from the edge of the sidewalk. In the event of a narrow sidewalk, the trainway can be cantilevered out over the street as shown. In each of these

General Electric's proposed Aerial Transport System.

DULLES INTERNATIONAL AIRPORT

arrangements there is no restriction of full use of the street,

In addition, new materials and methods of construction will make it possible to use fewer supporting towers. Cable-supported guideways (similar in principle to suspension bridges) can have 300-foot spans, as opposed to 75 feet for beam and column construction.

Suspended guideways offer three advantages: grade cross-ings, always a problem, are avoided; there is less likelihood of foreign objects being dropped, thrown, or blown onto the guideway; and there is less disruption of surface ac-tivities than with at-grade (surface) systems.

Naturally, such suspension-type systems need not be con-fined to elevated travel. In highly congested areas, they can be routed underground like any subway. And in suburban areas or between cities, the cars can travel at surface level. Obviously, however, when run in these modes, suspension systems lose some of their advantage over conventional rail systems.

Clearly, each suspension-type system must be evaluated on the basis of the problems, traffic requirements, etc. of the community it is intended to serve.

In general, rapid transit proposals and projects are con-centrated in large, established regional centers with present or future urban populations of more than 1.5 million people. It is well known even now that the larger the city, the higher the proportion of transit travel into and out of the downtown area.

In a number of cities, such as New York, Chicago, Newark, Philadelphia, Richmond, Boston, Atlanta, and Cleveland, from one-half to three-quarters of all persons entering the CBD do so by some form of rail transportation. A recent study indicated that peak-hour traffic congestion in a city can be cut to a tolerable level by reducing the number of

Coordinated use of land for rapid transit and cars in some city of the future.

autos entering the CBD by one-fourth. In one well-coordinated arrangement in Chicago, rapid transit carries 50 per cent more people than the four-lane expressway alongside it, yet adds only 10 per cent to the construction cost. The combination has worked so well that the city is building two more transit lines down the center of two other major expressways. The illustration shows how this might work in some city of the future.

One clever comment on the car vs. rail question was made by Dr. R. E. Packer, engineer and author. He said, "Every driver wants rapid transit—because he hopes it will remove the driver in front of him."

WITHDRAWN

J. W. Poynter Jr. H. S. Library From 33
1 . E. Grant St., Poynter Jr. High Library
Hillsboro, Oregon 97123

7669

The truth of the matter is that travel by public transportation is strongly conditioned by a number of factors which are *not* directly related to the quality of available service. Examples are level of family income, automobile ownership, and density of urban development. It has even been suggested that the American West was won by men on horseback, and that many men still have a similar feeling for their cars.

The question is, can these men (and women as well) be pried from their "saddles?" We have seen that innovation in rail systems offers some indication that they can. An important step is making a multi-mode system out of our various transportation modes. The stated objective of the New York Metropolitan Transportation Authority (MTA) is to provide better service by "meshing" all the services—subway, bus, commuter train, cars, and perhaps even aircraft.

There are other hopeful signs. One is that public funds for public transit, which was once thought to be strictly the province of private industry, have steadily increased. There is now a growing feeling that government must provide support. Now the question is not whether, but how much and what kind. In the last few years the DOT has advanced from strictly a supporting arm of research and development to the point where it now provides substantial grants for transit improvements. Money spent by the government on public transport however, is still far less than is spent on road construction. A number of municipal officials and legislators are urging that a "Transit Trust Fund," similar to the existing Highway Trust Fund, be set up to provide adequate funding for transit systems, which require very long lead times for planning and building. The BART system has been 14 years in the making and is not completed yet.

Rapid transit systems are being built or contemplated in a large number of cities around the world; in the U.S. these include Atlanta, Baltimore, Boston, Denver, Detroit, Houston, Las Vegas, Los Angeles, Miami, Pittsburgh, San Francisco, Seattle, and Washington, D.C. The types of system vary widely. Both Las Vegas and Pittsburgh, in spite of the difference in their size, are considering PRT-type systems. Boston and San Francisco, acting in cooperation, are buying what are called Light Rail Vehicles (LRV), but which turn out to be updated trolley cars! The 71-foot articulated (bend-in-the-middle) streetcars will be the first to be built in the U.S. since 1952. The articulation, widely used in Europe though not here, permits these longer vehicles to negotiate city-street turns so that a single motorman can "drive" more people. Articulation also permits uninterrupted passage through the cars.

But in most cases the systems involved are standard, though highly automated, train systems. DOT asked the rail and aerospace industries for ideas for a "state of the art" (SOAC) car. Interestingly, the Boeing Company has been designated systems manager. Two cars have already been built and are being tested at DOT's new High Speed Ground Test Center in Pueblo, Colorado. The objective is to provide a standard for industry—a single optimized design, using present-day technology, that will provide high performance (e.g., acceleration from 0–80 mph in just over one minute), standardized design (to facilitate cooperative purchase and thus lower prices), and lower "womb-to-tomb" cost. The cars are fast, comfortable, and quiet. One test rider "complained" that the one he was riding in was "too quiet."

DOT has also instituted a program to develop an Advanced Concept Train (ACT). It will be interesting to see what comes of it.

An important point to remember, however, is that transportation cannot be thought of only in terms of the hardware.

Lower fares and higher tolls for cars during peak riding hours, for example, would encourage the use of public transport. And perhaps public transport should in some way be used for other purposes as well; night deliveries of freight or mail might make the subways safer as well as more profitable. Perhaps the hard, knife-proof seats the New York MTA has had to put into its vehicles will have one advantage; it makes them easier to remove or stack out of the way to clear the space for cargo. Nor should this be considered an impractical idea. Airlines do it all the time.

Land-use approaches are also intimately involved. If we continue to spread out, as we have in our suburban communities, then public transport becomes less and less likely to be practicable. If the number of cars continues to grow at the current rapid rate, it may become necessary to set up zoning regulations that encourage concentration of people. This does not necessarily mean that people must live on top of one another. The objective is rather that sub-centers or satellite cities will be created, containing industry, recreation, and residential areas, so that outlying residents from various areas will have a single place to go to. Only then does public transport begin to make sense.

As the Regional Plan Association, a private group concerned with the New York-New Jersey-Connecticut region, put it: "The rational location of job opportunities can multiply the number of persons *choosing* to use buses and trains."*

In later chapters we will discuss other approaches to the commuter problem and to short-distance travel within the city center as well. In the meantime, let us see what rail-type transportation offers to the medium- and long-distance traveler of the future.

---

* *How to Save Urban America,* p. 10.

High Speed Ground Transportation

THE FIRST steam-powered train built expressly for rails ran in England in 1804. On the very first trip it carried ten tons of iron, five wagons, and seventy men. It took four hours to cover 9 1/2 miles, for a sparkling average of just over two miles an hour.

But it was a start, and by 1849 European express trains could hit 75 mph, a respectable speed even now. In 1893, the American locomotive 999 set a world's record: 100 mph. While this was exciting, what was going on in the American West was even more so. What red-blooded American youngster has not thrilled to the exploits of the brave railroaders? Who can doubt that it was the railroad which finally pried open the American West? Hard though it may be to believe, it was not until a century ago that the eastern and western coasts of the United States were directly linked by rail. It was on May 10, 1869, that the final, ceremonial golden spike was driven.

For a long time, the railroad was the ultimate in travel. And it grew quickly, not only in America, but also all over the world. England had 1,600 miles of rail by 1841, and 6,890 only ten years later. By the mid-1800's, some trains had become virtual hotels on wheels, with comfortable beds, chandeliers, thick carpets, velvet draperies, even libraries, and good food. (In America, at least, one had the choice of elk, antelope, buffalo, beefsteak, mutton, or grouse.)

But far more important was the question of trip time. The trip between the east and west coasts of the United States had once taken five to six months by wagon; it could be made in three months by fast clipper around Cape Horn. Suddenly, the journey could be made in five or six days! There was nothing to compare with it.

Now, a full century later, it takes three days—an improvement of only 100 per cent. Compared to the increased speeds of aircraft and even ships over their early days, this is hardly any improvement at all.

Problems of the Railroads

Of course, jets now make the trip in about five hours. Does this mean that, except for commuting purposes, the passenger train is doomed? For a number of years now, this has seemed to be the case. For the long-haul train it is almost certainly true, at least for the railroad train as we know it today. After a study of eleven western railroads, the Stanford Research Institute concluded that the long-haul, intercity passenger train "seems destined to disappear from the American scene."

Many railroad companies are delighted with this conclusion. Rising costs, dwindling traffic, and competition from other forms of transportation have put the squeeze on. Most lines make up their losses in passenger activities from freight income—trains still haul 40 per cent of the nation's goods.

In some cases the freight end of the business has not been enough to keep the railroad out of financial trouble. On June 20, 1970, Penn Central, the nation's largest railroad went bankrupt.

A year later the government, in an attempt to help the overall situation, set up AMTRAK, a semi-public corporation owned by the nation's railroads, to run passenger rail service in the United States—with financial help from the government. One of AMTRAK's first acts was to *cut* passenger service to about half what it had been before that. Nevertheless, the situation continues to deteriorate. Today, Penn Central is only one of six railroads in the northeast that are bankrupt—together these six railroads operate half the trackage in this populous region.

While it is unlikely that the railroad—at least in its present state of development—can ever regain its previous eminence, there are promising signs for the future. This is especially true for the medium-distance trip of 100 to 400 miles, which is today more often taken by car, bus, or plane.

The first two modes certainly don't help the highway situation. Even in the case of aircraft, highway travel is normally involved, i.e., getting to and from the airport by private car, bus, taxi, or limousine. There are only a few cities in the entire world where it is possible to get from city center to airport by rail.

Tokyo's monorail, the Brussels subway, and the Cleveland rail link are three exceptions. And, as part of a sweeping blueprint for expanding and consolidating New York City's mass-transit facilities, the Long Island Railroad may provide a fourth. A spur off the main line would make possible direct, 20-minute service from Manhattan to Kennedy International Airport. The trip is now an uncertain 30–60 minute car or bus ride, or an expensive 12–14 minute helicopter ride.

When looked at from the overall point of view, the question must not be, "How fast does the vehicle travel?" or even, "How long does it take to fly from New York to Washington?" Rather the question should be phrased, "How long does the trip take from door to door?"

By car, the trip from New York to Washington, D.C., is normally a hard five-hour drive. The plane trip is under an hour, but connections and local travel generally bring the total up to two and a half hours or so. Another problem with plane travel lies in a certain amount of undependability. As we have mentioned, traffic in the skies, particularly in the northeast, is not much better than on the ground.

Weather, too, can play havoc with plane schedules. It is not unusual to make the plane trip in lightning time and then circle the airport for half or three-quarters of an hour before being allowed to land. (This is similar to being stuck in a traffic jam on a highway leading into a city.)

The advantages offered by train travel are transportation from city center to city center, comfort, and dependability. If the schedule says arrival at 3 P.M., you can be fairly certain that that is the time you will get there—at least on the better railroads.

The problem with trains seems now to be speed, or lack of it. Let us return to the New York–Washington run. We figured the car trip for five hours, and the plane for two and a half. How about the train?

A conventional train might leave New York at 4:30 P.M., make four intermediate stops—at Newark, Philadelphia, Wilmington, and Baltimore—and arrive at the nation's capital at 8:05. This is just over three and a half hours. With additional connections at the ends of the trip, an average total might be four hours.

But these trains are limited to speeds of 80 mph. If train speeds could be raised to 100 mph, the train could arrive in Washington at 7:30; at 125 mph, it could arrive at 7:09; and at 150 mph, at 6:48. This last trip would take just over two hours; many commuters spend this much time getting to work every day.

The Super-Express

What are the prospects for such speeds? In other countries, they are very good; in the United States they are improving. But we must understand that there are two major aspects. One is the potential speed of a train under ideal conditions; the second is how fast the train can actually run on the existing roadbed.

In the U.S. the much heralded and very successful Metroliner, which provides excellent passenger service between New York and Washington, has a potential top speed of more than 150 mph. Unfortunately, track conditions limit it to a much lower speed. On the section between Washington and Baltimore it has been clocked at 93 mph. Even at that speed, there are sections of the trip where one feels one is riding a jackhammer.

It is extremely difficult to upgrade existing track; and replacing it is extremely expensive. The problems are alleviated slightly when building a new system, as the Japanese did in the run between Tokyo and Osaka. With completely new track, and considerable and constant maintenance work, the *Hikari* (lightning) trains make the 320-mile total run, with two intermediate stops, in three hours, for an average of over 100 mph.

TurboTrain on the Boston-New York run; in service since April 1969.

The northern part of the northeast corridor run—New York to Boston—presents a somewhat different set of problems. Here there are many more curves on the railroad line, and many parts are not electrified. Newly developed turbine-powered trains rather than electric Metroliners are being used on this line. It is significant that the TurboTrains, although built by Pullman-Standard (a train manufacturer), were developed by United Aircraft. Although the company guarantees a top speed of 160 mph, top speed has been held at 110 mph until now.

The engines are one of the most significant aspects of the new trains. They are light in weight but very powerful, having been developed originally for aircraft. Each power dome car contains from two to four of these engines, depending on the train's makeup and schedule. It is also equipped to pick up power from a third rail so that the train can operate in tunnels like those in Manhattan.

Other innovations are lightweight bodies and a new form of suspension described as *pendulous*. The system is intended to bank the train into the curves just as an aircraft does, rather than allowing the car bodies to try to lean outward as they normally do. This approach, along with a low center of gravity, enables the equipment to round the many curves on

42

this run at speeds 30 to 40 per cent higher than those of conventional trains.

In other countries, where train travel is more important than it is here, more is happening. The French, Germans, Italians, and British are all hard at work on high-speed trains. The French have already built and are testing a 185-mph TurboTrain. The German Federal Railroad has approved plans for construction of 600 miles of electrified, high-speed routes designed for eventual passenger train speeds of 185 mph, although the first phase of the program will use 155-mph trains.

It is important to understand that it is not just a matter of increasing the propulsive power—indeed this is probably the least of the problem. Oscillation, jackhammering, and braking problems are all difficult to solve at high speeds. For example, some of the trains are light weight—which aids in rapid acceleration and low energy consumption, but creates a problem with wheel contact forces. If any kind of film forms on the rails, the wheels may end up spinning rather than driving the train.

The British are working on what they call the Advanced Passenger Train (APT). An important aspect of the APT is that it is designed to operate on existing trackage. Among other things this means that a 155-mph train must be able to stop in the same distance as a current 100-mph train.

This creates a problem because the energy of braking that must be dissipated goes up as the square of the speed. Straight frictional braking no longer is possible, and water-cooled and electrical braking are being considered. In the latter, the current in the electric motors is reversed, so that they act as brakes. As in the United Aircraft TurboTrain, light-weight gas turbines are being used as the power plant. Such matters as aerodynamic design, and pressure waves as

British Rail's Advanced Passenger Train (APT-E).

the train enters a tunnel or passes another train head on, also become extremely tricky.

The APT uses a powered tilt system, in which sensors measure lateral (side-to-side) acceleration and cause the train body to tilt inward during turns to minimize discomfort to passengers. The TurboTrain does this too, but because it depends on the centrifugal force exerted, the system is not as fast-acting or responsive as the British APT. The system can also prevent tilting due to side winds and to passengers getting on and off at stations. British Railways maintains that on new, high-grade track the train should be capable, with some small modification, of 250 mph—assuming other problems can be solved. For one thing, operation would have to be completely automated, and electronic obstacle-detection systems will be needed because of extended stopping distances of one to several miles. They will be located along the tracks and tied in with the on-board controls.

The British are hoping that the APT will not have to charge premium fares. They point to the previous five years on the London-Manchester run, during which annual seats sold rose from one to two million. Six hundred thousand of these were new traffic generated by better train service. While increased speed is by no means the only factor involved in improving service (in the London-Manchester run the most important factor was increased frequency of service), there is no doubt that higher speeds are important. The high-speed trains provide more passenger-miles in the same time, while at the same time becoming more desirable as a mode of travel. British Railways uses a rule of thumb of one to one and a half per cent increase in business for every one per cent increase in speed. Thus a 50 per cent increase in speed can generate as much as 75 per cent more business.

Both gas-turbine and electrical APTs are being built and evaluated. Because the APT is as new as it is, a so-called High Speed Train (HST)—at 125 mph it might more aptly be called a medium speed train—will be introduced first.

The basic form of structure in conventional track has not changed in over a century. For the higher speed APTs, some new form of track arrangement will be necessary. British Railways is experimenting with a solid, continously laid slab of concrete as a support for the rails. This can be laid to quite tight specifications and, more important, seems to maintain the specifications as opposed to conventional track which must be continuously monitored and adjusted for faster trains.

The technology of steel wheels on steel tracks is being pushed hard, perhaps to its ultimate end. With increase of speed, the problem of driving and braking, depending as it does on the friction between smooth wheels and rails, meets definite limits (the question of just what these limits are has not yet been definitely decided). For example, high-speed

45

racing cars sometimes use airfoils to force them *down* in order for the tires to maintain a good grip on the surface. This is necessary because, at high speeds, the vehicle itself begins to act like an airfoil. At these speeds, even small surface irregularities on the tracks produce vertical motions which reduce the firmness of contact.

New and Unconventional Systems

All of this brings us to the next part of our discussion, namely unconventional ground transportation systems. One major area of investigation is a possible substitute for the wheel. There are actually several aspects to the question, which normally resolve themselves into the areas of suspension, propulsion, and braking. The last two can be, and often are, considered together.

Methods of suspension for high-speed vehicles fall into three general classes: mechanical contact, fluid pressure, and magnetic forces.

The first, *mechanical contact,* refers to sliding or rolling members. Sliding surfaces are definitely out because of the great amount of frictional resistance and heat involved. By rolling members, we mean wheels, of course, but also rollers or any other similar kind of device. The point is to keep an open mind and not eliminate any approach that might prove useful.

Nevertheless, there is a feeling that this general class of suspension may not be practical for high-speed travel. Professors W. W. Seifert and R. J. Hanson of the Massachusetts Institute of Technology point out that there is a tendency for various "dynamic instabilities" to occur as speed is increased. Thus, they maintain, in the speed range of 200 mph and up, conventional suspension technology is almost certain to be inadequate even when vehicles are operated over the smoothest guideways.

As with the mechanical contact class, there are also various approaches to *fluid suspension*. Among them are air cushions, air bearings, and aerodynamic lifting surfaces. In the last case, the vehicle is simply flying. This, in combination with a track, can cause trouble. For example, a gust of wind might throw a vehicle against the track, or even into a nose dive. In a plane there is room to overcome such deviations. Not here. However, we shall see in a moment that this effect actually becomes useful when used in conjunction with the air-cushion mode. Air bearings and air pads have not found application because of the high pressures required and other difficult technical problems.

Air-Cushion Vehicles

On the other hand, there is a great deal of activity in the air-cushion field. A number of Tracked Air Cushion Vehicles (TACVs, pronounced *tack-vees*) have already been built and are being tested.

Before going into these, however, we must make a slight detour and discuss propulsion problems first. The earlier version of TACVs generally used propellers or even rockets to generate forward motion. Such forms were needed because there is no mechanical contact, namely wheels, between train and guideway. There are problems with rockets and propellers however. Among them are noise, heat blast, vibration, and air pollution (especially in tunnels).

A more advanced approach has been taking shape. Let us recall that an electric motor generally has a central part, the rotor, which spins inside an outer case, the stator. In the so-called linear motor, one half of an electric motor is in effect opened up and laid out flat along the guideway while the other half is in the vehicle. When electricity is passed through the winding of the system, the vehicle is pulled along the track in very much the same way that a normal rotor is moved around its axis, by electromagnetic forces. In addition to the fact that thrust is produced without any physical contact, linear motors provide other advantages. These include lack of moving parts, less weight in the vehicle (saving both weight and space), no noise or vibration, no pollution along the route (assuming the electric power used is not generated aboard the vehicle, but is picked up along the way), and excellent performance. And, finally, because there are no centrifugal forces caused by spinning members, speed of the motor is virtually unlimited.

The linear motor (at least the type we are discussing here) is often called a linear induction motor, or LIM. The reason, again, has to do with how a typical electric motor works. That is, when current starts to flow through the windings

Linear Induction Motor (LIM).

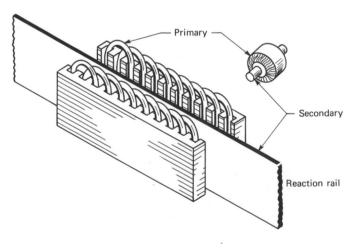

48

of the stator, currents are *induced* in the windings of the rotor; these interact with magnetic fields produced in the stator and produce the desired rotational motion. In the linear motor, currents are induced in a reaction rail (see illustration), which is so called because it transfers the thrust reaction to the ground. The reaction rail may also be used to help provide lateral guidance for the vehicle.

Let us see now how the LIM is being used.

Two research vehicles of the more advanced American TACV systems are shown. They are intended for different purposes. One, the UTACV (U for urban), is to be a relatively short-range, medium-speed, LIM-driven version which might carry passengers at 150 mph from city center to outlying airport or suburb. This 60-passenger vehicle features a noise level half that of an average automobile. If all goes well we might see such a system linking the new Dallas/Fort Worth Airport with these two cities in the near future.

The other, the TACRV (R for research), is intended for longer hauls, probably city center to city center. The objective here is a speed of perhaps 300 mph. The TACRV has been called the most sophisticated ground vehicle ever built in the United States. Two stages are envisioned. In stage one (see page 50) the vehicle will be propelled as well as levitated by expelled air. Maximum air gap for the air cushions is about one inch, with cushion air supplied by three turbofan engines. In stage two the electric propulsion system will consist of two 4,000-hp linear motors. An important aspect of the LIM is superior performance, which is clearly seen in the following comparison. Under aero propulsion, the vehicle can accelerate to 125 mph in 2 1/2 minutes; with two LIMS, it will take only 1 1/4 minutes to reach 300 mph. By the same token, electromagnetic braking ("reversing the engines") is also more efficient.

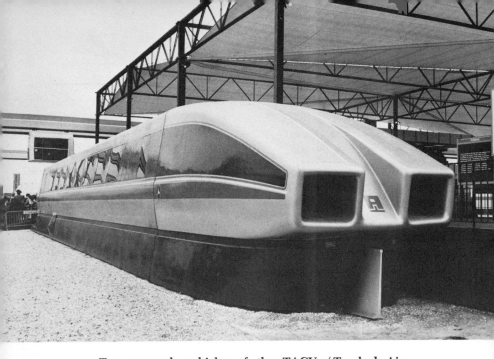

Two research vehicles of the TACV (Tracked Air Cushion Vehicle) system being tested at DOT's High Speed Ground Test Center. Top: UTACV (Urban Tracked Air Cushion Vehicle); bottom: TACRV (Tracked Air Cushion Research Vehicle).

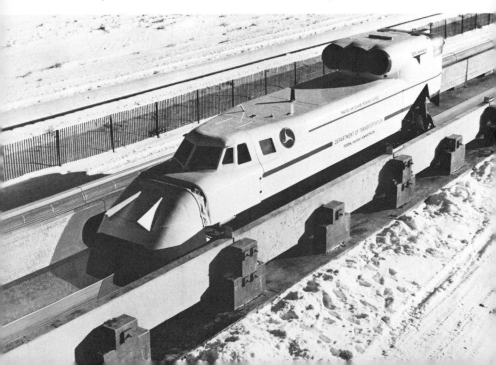

The two vehicles have different suspension systems. The UTACV uses chamber-type air cushions, as opposed to higher pressure, smaller, peripheral jet air cushions in the TACRV. This will permit comparison of the qualities of each. Both vehicles are to be tested at the DOT's new High Speed Ground Test Center.

Current collection, which could be a problem since there is no contact between vehicle and guideway, will probably be handled, at least at first, by an electric line running along the guideway and a flexible connector or arm from the vehicle that slides or rolls along it. To get around the complications inherent in this, DOT is also looking into the possibility of generating the electricity on board the craft. The stirling cycle (piston) and Brayton cycle (turbine) engines show great promise.

The French have also been very active in TACV work. They have actually begun work on a line that will connect

Prototype of 80-passenger TACV in operation near Orleans, France; has reached speeds of 265 mph.

the La Defense station of the Paris Regional (rail) Express to a new satellite community approximately 15 miles outside Paris.

Since the British appear confident that wheeled systems can be made to work at speeds even up to 250 mph, one might wonder whether it is worth bothering with these new and relatively untried methods. And the British have indeed scrapped their TACV project because they feel wheels *will* work at high speeds. But proponents of the TACVs point to lower construction and maintenance costs, minimal noise and maximal riding comfort, high propulsion efficiency, and good acceleration, deceleration, and braking properties.

Emergency braking of a 300-mph train presents some interesting problems. Among the devices considered are electromagnetic braking (already mentioned), cutting off the suspension power so that the vehicle drops down and drags on skids, and even an emergency chute that pops open in the back.

Because of the low requirements for smoothness and alignment of the guideway surface (clearly the word "rail" is no longer applicable), and the fact that the load is not concentrated in very small areas as it is on wheels, the construction costs for air-cushion guideways can be much lower than for any other form of ground transportation discussed so far. Elimination of the heavy steel wheels and wheel trucks can save as much as 10,000 to 15,000 pounds in the overall weight of the vehicle.

There is an additional advantage to ACVs. Thanks to the spreading out of the air cushion, the vehicle is supported across a large surface, rather than just at two ends, as in a normal train or bus. Hence the construction need not be as rigid, leading to lighter vehicles.

A slightly different, and very interesting, approach has

A French Urba car.

been taken in another system designed by the French. In a manner similar to the SAFEGE system described earlier, the Urba also operates as a suspended system. And like the other TACVs we have described, it too is an air-suspended, LIM-driven type. But there is a basic difference in its suspension system. The Urba design makes use of suction air cushions for suspension—in other words, vacuum cleaners! These lower the air pressure at the suspension points and atmospheric air pressure then supports the vehicle. Lower air pressure means quieter and perhaps more efficient operation. Like the SAFEGE system, Urba uses a slotted box guideway. Although Urba has been designed for Urban operation, the negative air-pressure system should have application for higher speeds as well.

There is one final possibility in the ACV class. This one

uses a series of air nozzles in the track to drive the vehicle. The air in the jets is expanded by means of electric arcs triggered by the arrival of the vehicle. The same air is used for both propulsion and suspension. While this is also true in ACVs, in this M.I.T. system, no fans, propellers, or motors are needed.

Magnetic Suspension Systems

We turn now to *magnetic suspension systems.* This system might be compared to the repulsion experienced when you try to bring together two bar magnets with north poles facing.

Magnetic levitation ("maglev") systems are less well along than the air-cushion types, mainly because very powerful fields are necessary to provide the required lifting forces. Developments in the science of low temperatures, however, have made such an approach possible.

Under normal conditions, very high electric currents, needed to energize the powerful electromagnets, create high temperatures. Thus, much of the input power is lost in the form of heat. Conversely, at very low temperatures (and I do mean *low*—on the order of –450° F.), metals become superconductive. That is, they offer no resistance at all to an electric current, and so there are no losses. At these cryogenic temperatures a current, once induced, can circulate for years with virtually no power loss. (Permanent magnets are a possibility, but for a practical system the power required far surpasses the capability of any known materials. A powerful enough magnet could be made but would be impossibly heavy.)

Several configurations are possible and work is being carried out mainly in Japan, Germany, and the United States.

One type of layout, being studied at Stanford Research Institute under a contract from DOT, is shown. The same magnetic force that lifts the vehicle can also be used to keep it centered; if a train tended to drift to one side, the repelling magnetic force on that side of the guideway would increase and tend to keep the vehicle centered. In the arrangement shown, the vehicle is supported by rubber tires at

Stanford Research Institute Maglev vehicle.

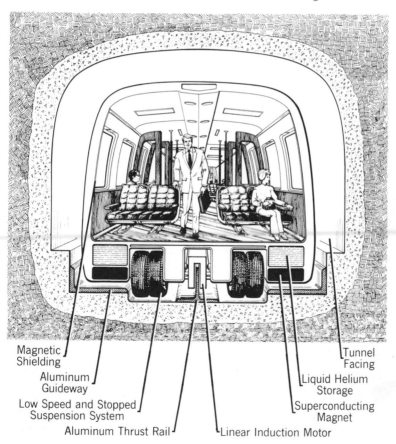

Magnetic Shielding

Aluminum Guideway

Low Speed and Stopped Suspension System

Aluminum Thrust Rail

Linear Induction Motor

Superconducting Magnet

Liquid Helium Storage

Tunnel Facing

This Japanese magnetically suspended, four-passenger research vehicle has 'flown" at 26 mph 4" above the test track.

low speeds or when stopped. As speed increases, electro-magnets on its lower surface cause current to flow in the aluminum guideway below, as in an LIM. These currents build up magnetic fields that repel the magnets on the vehicle and the vehicle "takes off," though not more than about a foot. This is more than the clearance used in ACVs, and therefore requirements for construction of the guideway can be less stringent. The greater lift will also be useful if non-enclosed guideways are used, in terms of operation over snow, ice, and debris.

Quieter operation is also possible due to lack of the fans or jets needed in ACV operation. And finally, it is believed that maglev systems will need less overall power than ACVs.

In the Japanese approach superconducting coils in the vehicle induce eddy currents in the track bed. A small four-passenger research vehicle of this type has already been "flown."

The Germans, farthest ahead of all, have taken yet another approach. Their most advanced system uses attractive rather than repelling forces—the guideway magnets are above those of the vehicle. In this system a smaller gap clearance (about a half inch) can be used, which means that less power is needed to keep the vehicle suspended; but it also means that tighter tolerances must be maintained. There is, too, the possibility that the attracting surfaces might clamp together if allowed to meet. To prevent this, a fast-acting electronic "servo-controlled" system is used that rapidly varies the current going through the coils to vary the magnetic forces as needed. An advantage of this type of system is that no "land-

Krauss-Maffei Transrapid Experimental Vehicle and Guideway. The vehicle is magnetically suspended and LIM-propelled.

ing gear" is needed, since the forces act even while the vehicle is at rest.

An American company, Rohr Industries, has so much faith in the maglev approach that it has produced, with its own money, a low-speed magnetically levitated vehicle, which has been named ROMAGTM. The company is now working on a second-generation vehicle. Rohr's board chairman, Burton Raynes, predicts that fifty years from now half of all passenger traffic will be supported by the magnetic levitation.

Clearly, one final advantage of the maglev approach is that it could share a number of components with the LIMs. This would provide obvious advantages in terms of size, weight, and cost of the overall system.

So far we have been more or less loafing along at a few hundred miles an hour. In the next chapter we begin to speed things up a bit.

4

Tunnels
and Tubes

On December 26, 1947, two friends and I were standing in Grand Central Station, waiting for the train to pull in that would take us north to Saranac Lake for a vacation. Since that was more than 25 years ago, I don't remember all the details, but a number of things are etched clearly in my mind. I know we waited several hours before the train even came into the station, and several more before it pulled out. We arrived at our destination 12 hours late.

The problem? A raging snowstorm was in the process of dumping several feet of snow all along the northeast. Planes and most cars, buses, and trucks gave up quickly. The trains apparently got through, but not without a mighty struggle. The subways ran—and pretty much on time. I can vouch for this because we got to the station by subway.

The moral is clear. The only way to prevent a recurrence of collapses of our transportation system is to *put transporta-*

tion underground, or in some kind of enclosed guideway.
Nor is snow the only weather problem. Fog, rainstorms,
hail, sleet, and even tornados and hurricanes all cause problems at one time or another in all parts of the United States.

But there is a further reason. Clearly, ground speeds of
100 mph or more call for exclusive rights-of-way—rails, for
example. A car traveling at 100 mph or more is normally a
sure candidate for trouble. As the speeds of ground systems
continue to increase, safety as well as all-weather considerations will make a move to enclosed guideways absolutely
necessary.

It is worth mentioning that over the years rail systems
have proved to be about the safest way to travel. During
the period 1963 through 1972, railroad passenger trains averaged only 1.47 passenger deaths per billion passenger miles
traveled; air fatalities averaged 1.71; buses averaged 1.95;
and cars and taxis averaged 22.6, or 15 times higher than
the rail figure. (In all fairness, however, it should also be
noted that while the automotive figure has been going down
in recent years, the railroad figure has been rising. The
1972 figures were, respectively, 19 and 5.3!)

Nevertheless, speeds of several hundred miles an hour
are unthinkable unless the trains are also protected from
snow and ice and from objects falling into or crossing their
path.

Almost any of the systems described in the last chapter
could be used in a tube or tunnel. But there are problems.
No matter how streamlined the vehicle may be, it still acts
like a piston in a tube. Clearly the piston must be a very
leaky one, or pressure buildup would finally prevent the
craft from moving at all. At high speeds, a great deal of air
per unit time must move from front to rear of the vehicle
through the space that separates it from the tube. This leads
to problems with air resistance and heat buildup.

60

Propulsion and Suspension

An interesting proposal, made by Dr. J. V. Foa of the Rensselaer Polytechnic Institute, is to *use* this air in the propulsion scheme. In essence, thrust is generated by continuously transferring the air immediately in front of the vehicle to its rear. This is very similar to what happens in a jet engine, and indeed the vehicle itself can be regarded as the central body of a jet engine, the outer shroud or case of which is represented by the wall of the tube.

As the air is drawn into the "engine," it is heated; it then expands and escapes out the rear. This is the action. The vehicle is driven forward by the inevitable reaction. (Newton's third law of motion: Every action has an equal and opposite reaction.)

At very high speeds, the air is *forced* into the "engine," but the principle remains the same. The tube-vehicle system may thus be viewed as operating like a jet engine with no or very little drag. Although officially known as Project Tubeflight, the system has been nicknamed the Air Gulper.

Current technology calls for powering the craft with a conventional gas turbine engine. But this leaves us with the problem of noxious fumes, which are corrosive as well as dangerous in closed spaces. Furthermore, the craft must carry its own fuel supply, as well as air for breathing, which whittles down the potential payload.

Dr. Foa's system uses a large-clearance air-cushion suspension system, with at least several feet between vehicle and wall. This clearance is necessary to facilitate movement of the air from front to back.

An important advantage of the large clearance, says Dr. Foa, is the freedom of the vehicle to tilt itself to the correct angle of bank in every turn, regardless of the speed at which the turn is negotiated. In principle, this is the same

Dr. J. V. Foa's tubeflight vehicle nicknamed the "Air Gulper." Inside, passengers seated two by two would be separated by a center aisle; television might bring them news, films or views of the area they are passing through.

system as the pendulous suspension system used in the United Aircraft TurboTrain. It adds greatly to the comfort and safety of the passengers and also contributes to the economy of the guideway, since it permits greater tolerances in building and tighter curvatures in turns. This latter factor makes it easier to avoid difficult or expensive terrain.

However, the large clearance makes use of the linear electric motor—the most desirable candidate for propulsion—difficult, for the larger the gap between stator and "rotor," the lower the efficiency of the system. Suspended wires and third rails do not lend themselves to use at really high speeds.

An interesting possibility is to use high frequency, or microwave, energy. Because of its high frequency, such energy travels more efficiently in tubes (commonly called waveguides) than in wires. By choosing the proper frequency, it is possible to use the system's tube itself as the waveguide! Hence, energy can be beamed to the vehicle for propulsion and perhaps suspension and communication as well.

The principle has been demonstrated many times. For example, a five-pound helicopter model has been kept aloft by microwave energy transmitted from the ground. Also, since the energy will essentially "fill" the tube, the effect of any rolling motions of the vehicle during banking turns will not interfere with the power supply.

With support from the Office of High Speed Transportation, Dr. Foa has constructed a 2,000-foot tunnel to test his models. "Flights" of the models are being made to obtain information on propulsion and aerodynamics.

One of the propulsion methods being tested is a development of Dr. Foa's. Basically, it involves the ejection of whirling air jets. These form a vortex, or whirlpool, at the rear of the vehicle. The result is high-velocity streams of air spiraling around the vehicle, and dragging the resisting masses of air along with them.

A drawing of such a propulsion scheme is shown on the next page, along with an actual photo of the fluid-bladed fan or propeller. In the photo, water has been used as the fluid to provide "visibility."

While current efforts are directed toward the 350–400 mph range, higher speeds are also possible, although they may require yet more futuristic propulsion schemes. One is an application of a relatively new field with the jawbreaking name, *magnetogasdynamics*. Here the interaction of charged gases and magnetic fields can be used to provide propulsion. The idea is still in the conceptual stage, but the

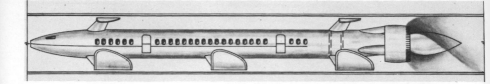

**Spiraling jets
of air drive the
tubeflight vehicle
forward.**

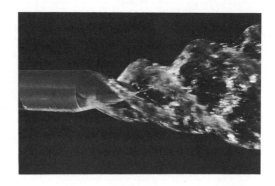

principle has to do with the fact that movement of charged
gases is similar to the flow of electrons through a wire.

In another system, the tube vehicle would operate in an
atmosphere of saturated water vapor. The idea is to get
around the aerodynamic drag problem by condensing the
vapor in front of the craft, thus shrinking the vapor and making it easier to get it out of the way. The liquid is then evap-
orated again at the rear. In this process, it expands and drives
the vehicle forward.

Which, if any, of these systems eventually becomes operational depends upon the outcome of the many studies now
in progress. One advantage common to all systems, where
air or vapor is used in a tube, shows up in the braking process. Clearly, this is an important factor in a craft traveling

several hundred miles an hour. In Tubeflight, no sooner is power to the engine shut off than the "piston" characteristic mentioned earlier comes to our aid. That is, the craft rapidly piles up air in front of it and slows down. At high speeds, the action is very rapid. Once the speed has been reduced to a low enough point, conventional friction forces can bring the vehicle to a stop.

Nevertheless, to obtain really high speeds, and for other reasons that will become clear shortly partial or full evacuation of the entire tube (creating a vacuum) must be considered. The most obvious system would use LIMs combined with magnetic suspension. As a matter of fact, the Rohr people have proposed a magnetically suspended, 2,000 mph "SST" (Super Sonic Train!) that would carry 80 passengers through an underground evacuated tunnel.

But there are other approaches. A fascinating alternative has been proposed by L. K. Edwards. This is essentially the gravity-vacuum system Andrew Mann used for his trip to Oakland in our Prologue.

Let's look first at the vacuum aspect of this proposal. Edwards points out that drag forces due to air resistance, even at present railroad speeds, are considerable, and that they increase as the square of the speed. At aircraft speeds, the movement of the air in a tube becomes prohibitive. (Even though the air in the Foa system is being used for propulsion, it is still moving from front to rear. The evaporation system is still purely theoretical.)

"Given the requirement for external power plants to remove the air from the tube," says Edwards, "why not make these the sole source of propulsive power for the train?"

It is only necessary to admit air at normal pressure behind the train by a system of valves. The higher pressure will force the train to move forward toward the region of lower pressure. Toward the end of the trip, it is only necessary to reverse the procedure—that is, to admit air in front of the train, to make it slow down.

There are several interesting differences between this system and those described earlier. For one thing, the concept of streamlining goes right out the window. The simplest and most efficient design calls for the front and back of the train to be perfectly flat, as shown. When sea-level pressure is applied to the roughly 10,000 square inches of either end of the train, a total propulsive (or braking) force of 140,000 pounds, or 70 tons, results. At 50 mph, this matches the pulling power of five large locomotives and provides ample acceleration capability.

Air can continue to push with this force at speeds as great as 200 mph. "At this point," says Edwards, "the effective power is 70,000 horsepower." Yet the only power plant required for a 450-mile northeast corridor system is a bank of four 2,500 hp (horse power) electric motors at one or two points along the tube—a maximum of 20,000 hp.

How can this be? Are we finally getting something for nothing? Not at all, for the motors are working continuously, while the train is only being accelerated for about two minutes.

This is the principle of the pneumatic catapult. Energy produced by a low horsepower engine and compressor is stored over a period of time for release in seconds.

In a sense then, reports Edwards, the tube train will be the world's longest catapult. However, the acceleration, instead of being very rapid, will be quite gradual. As a matter of fact, passengers won't even need seat belts. The acceleration will be carefully controlled by a series of valves that will open and close as the train passes through the tunnel.

The use of pneumatic systems is not new. Pneumatic delivery tubes were once widely used in department stores. They are still in use in large libraries and various other in-

Tunnels
and Tubes

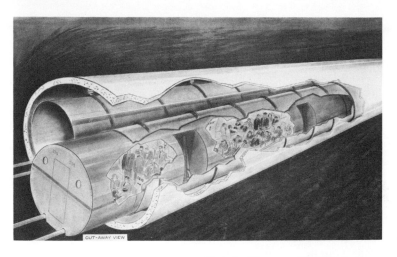

Gravity Vacuum Transit System.

stitutions, such as the Paris post office system. A pneumatic passenger system was actually built in Ireland as far back as 1840. But the materials available were not up to the job. A long leather flap, used to seal the long slot by means of which propulsion was accomplished, fell victim to the weather and to rats!

New York City's first subway, built in 1870 and a block long, was of the pneumatic type. A blower propelled the 18-passenger test car through the tunnel in one direction, and then reversed to "suck" it back. It was tested for a whole year and was a popular attraction all the while. But a full size system was never built. The elevated railroads got the nod and became the standard for a number of years.

While Edwards' propulsion system is still far in advance of anything we have now, his suspension system is even more surprising. He suggests the use of steel wheels and rails! His feeling, which is supported by Dr. William C. Ronan, is that this is the most efficient system considered so far.

67

For example, steel wheels moving on steel rails encounter far less resistance than rubber tires rolling and flexing on pavement. It takes 7 1/2 times more force to move a loaded vehicle with rubber tires than it does to move an equally loaded steel-wheeled railroad car. The more advanced systems such as air and magnetic suspension, require a continual, additional expenditure of power.

Edwards also says (in clear disagreement with prevailing opinion) that steel wheels will work quite well at speeds up to 500 mph—with some precautions and special adaptation, such as the use of a specially designed floated tube. It is also worth recalling that jet-propelled autos, traveling on the Bonneville Salt Flats, have attained speeds of more than 600 mph—with rubber tires!

Tunnels

Although a surface tube would work as well as a tunnel, Edwards suggests the latter, for several reasons. He says that a tube on or above the surface would be an "unsightly nuisance." He adds that a reasonable degree of straightness would call for many bridges and tunnels.

The Japanese system, for instance, includes some 40 miles of tunnels (a full eighth of its total length), although it is supposed to be a surface system. Since the tube system is intended for downtown-to-downtown trips, some portion of it would have to be underground anyway.

Furthermore, tunneling does not, or need not, disrupt surface activities in congested areas. Bores can be run below the network of water mains, power lines, sewers, and building foundations, eliminating the need for expensive and time-consuming detours. Work in underground facilities progresses steadily in all seasons. Below a certain depth the temperature is always above freezing so tunneling can be continued in all kinds of weather.

In addition to having his train used in a corridor-type system, i.e., for medium and long distances, Edwards would also like to see it used for urban transportation. However, his pneumatic system (which could be put in a surface tube) would not suffice for the latter. That is, for shorter trips and heavier, longer trains, pneumatic power alone could not provide the acceleration required. Nor could it, apparently, for speeds above 200 mph, even in the longer distance applica- tions.

We mentioned earlier that the Montreal Metro uses gravity to aid in accelerating its trains. Edwards proposes to obtain such "free speed" in a similar manner, though on a much larger scale. Clearly, this kind of system can only operate in tunnels.

Edwards points out that once the decision is made to put the system into a tunnel, it would cost very little more to slope the sides downward on both sides of each station. If the slope is steep enough, e.g., a maximum depth of 4,300 feet for an eight-mile distance, the trip—using gravity alone! —would take 2.1 minutes. The vehicle, in other words, would act like the bob of a pendulum. In the absence of any fric tional forces, the vehicle could swing back and forth between the stations forever.

A passenger in such a train would feel absolutely no front-to-back acceleration; he could stand up and even pour water with no trouble at all. There would be a small feeling of vertical acceleration, which would be similar to but far less than that experienced on a roller coaster. Nevertheless, such a slope would be too steep near the stations for a practical system. Hence the slope is smoothed out or flattened at the ends. The maximum depth of the tunnel becomes 3,000 feet and, with pneumatic propulsion, the trip takes 3.2 minutes.

Returning now to long-distance transportation, a very curious effect is seen to arise. Suppose we *could* bore a hole straight through the center of the earth and out the other side. And suppose we dropped a rock down the hole. What would happen?

The rock would start off with zero speed and maximum acceleration, or 32 feet per second per second. As it fell, the speed of the rock would increase, but at a continually diminishing rate; for with each foot of fall, there would be less of the earth attracting it from the front and more attracting it from the rear.

By the time it reached the center of the earth, the speed of the rock would be at a maximum (about five miles per *second*). But its acceleration would be zero, for now the gravitational attraction in front and back would balance. As it sped through the center point, conditions would reverse. Now there would be more of the earth behind it than in front, and it would begin to slow up. By the time it reached the other side, its speed would be exactly zero mph once again.

Total elapsed time for the trip: 42 minutes. Energy expended: none.

Now, assuming no one caught the stone, back it would go. Forty-two minutes later, it would appear on our side of the earth again.

The point, of course, is that the hole could be a tunnel and the stone could be a vehicle. We could load the vehicle with 10,000 people or as many tons of cargo. The trip would take the same time and our cost for energy would be no greater.

Total elapsed time for the round trip is a little more than 84 minutes, or just about the time it takes an astronaut traveling at 18,000 mph to circle the earth! This is not a coincidence. Multiply the speed of the stone at the center of the earth by 3,600 (to convert miles per second to mph) and you have a speed of 18,000 mph! This is the speed at which a satellite must be fired horizontally to give it a circular orbit around the earth, just above its surface. (We are, of course, ignoring the effects of air resistance.)

If the satellite (or passenger rocket) were fired off at a higher speed, away it would go into space. So the fastest time one could make in going halfway around the world in this manner is 42 minutes—at an enormous expenditure of fuel.

If, however, we could build our tunnel through the earth, we could get there with no expenditure of energy. If we were in a great rush, all we would need to do is to use some form of propulsion to accelerate us during the first half of our trip. A small, constant acceleration during this period would cut the time considerably. However, the vehicle would then have to be slowed down artificially during the second half. With this technique, we could conceivably make the trip in ten or fifteen minutes.

Will the earth one day be crisscrossed with tunnels like those of earthworms under a lawn? Perhaps. But there are a few small problems that must be solved first. One is a fiery heat at great depths. Another is air resistance, but that could be overcome if the air is removed from the tunnel.

There is also a pressure problem. A vertical, square-inch "rod" of atmosphere weighs about 15 pounds. This is the cause of our atmospheric pressure of 15 pounds per square inch. You have undoubtedly felt the pressure buildup on your eardrums as you dove down into water only ten feet deep. This is simply the weight of the water above you.

As one moves down farther into the earth, the pressure builds up rapidly. At very high pressures, strange things begin to happen. At a pressure of 150,000 pounds per square inch, graphite—black, soft, and greasy—changes to diamond.

Unfortunately, the pressure at the center of the earth is 300 times higher still. Diamond changes *back* to a soft material—indeed, any known substance turns into a kind of thick liquid. But there is one thing I have learned in writing this book, and that is *not* to say that something can't be done.

Suppose we didn't have anyone we wanted to visit directly opposite us. Suppose we wished, instead, to go only a quarter of the way around (or through) the earth, say to England. What is the situation then?

Of course, the heat and pressure are cut considerably. But will we still get a free ride? Yes, but now it is more like traveling down an incline than falling down a straight vertical tube. Gravity still acts to pull the vehicle toward the midpoint of the tunnel, although with proportionately less force. So, while we are traveling a shorter distance, we are moving at a slower speed. The result is that the time of the trip remains the same, 42 minutes.

Indeed, theoretically the time for a free trip through a straight tube to any place on earth is 42 minutes.

Tunneling Techniques

Oddly, cutting a perfectly straight tunnel has long been a major problem. There are no rulers or straight edges that can be counted on for long distances. A pinpoint of light can be used, but the light spreads. Laser light, however, spreads very little. It is interesting to note that one of the first successful applications of the laser has been in drilling a straight tunnel. A giant tunnel borer maintains arrow straightness with a unique laser-beam guidance system. So we have one of the problems licked.

A different problem is that of cutting through hard materials. The laser may just prove useful here, too. Experiments have shown that bursts of laser light weaken rock to a point where it can practically be dug out like soil. However, the power required thus far is much too high for practical use.

Compare this to the ancient Roman method, which was quite similar in principle. One of their tunnels was cut through 3,000 feet of solid rock. To do this, they first heated the rock with fire, then doused it with cold water to make it split. Finally, they hacked away at it with hand tools.

Other approaches, aside from the brute force methods of drilling, cutting, and blasting, are also being investigated. Among them are *flame jets*, currently being used in quarries and taconite mines; *electron beams;* high-pressure *water jets,* also called water cannons (after all, water did cut the Grand Canyon); and *chemicals*: a substantial weakening of rock samples has been achieved with the application of relatively inexpensive chemical agents.

The study of tunneling techniques is considered an important part of the government's research program. One hope, incidentally, is that the costs of tunnels can be shared. The U.S. Postal Service is interested and freight, too, can be shipped this way, perhaps in odd hours. In addition, the outer shell of the tunnel can be used for the transportation of petroleum products, water and/or chemicals.

One other point: Energy will be the key to our technological future, as it has been to our past and present. Vast amounts of energy will have to be "shipped" from place to place as energy requirements continue to increase. What more logical way is there than through our tunnel?

As a matter of fact, new techniques have been developed for transporting solid materials through pipelines as well. At this point the dividing line between tunnels and pipelines begins to get a little fuzzy. Size and "cargoes" are probably the only real distinction. Pipelines even today are a major mode of freight transportation. Oil pipelines carry one-fifth of the total ton-miles of intercity freight in the United States. They are quiet, efficient, and non-polluting. Transcontinental Gas Pipe Line has proposed to the U.S. Postal Service a new type of pipeline to move the mail.

All of this could be combined, with the various users sharing the admittedly high cost of a tunnel. DOT is studying the feasibility of such a multi-use transportation and utility tunnel along the northeast corridor.

A recent report to Congress on the progress being made in the corridor program stated that tunnels are sure to be important to any future ground transportation system, not only for the reasons we have given, but also because the cost of surface routes through urban centers is already in some cases above the cost of tunneling.

Finally, the Greek city planner Constantinos Doxiados believes that the pressure of expanding population may force us to place the whole system of mechanical transportation underground. Thus, the surface of the earth would be left free for people once again.

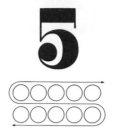

The Road Ahead

IN THE DAYS when the railroad was king, many cities literally grew up around the stations. This made sense since railroads, the only fast and reliable means of transportation, were practically the lifelines of the cities.

When the automobile came into being, it was "logical" for the highways—which grew out of local roads—to follow the pattern and run right through the hearts of the cities. Not so very long ago an automobile driver traveling from New York City to Washington, D.C., had to pass through the center of Baltimore over a narrow "main" road packed with cars, buses, and trucks. (Nationwide traffic studies have shown that 60 to 80 per cent of all motorists using downtown streets during rush hours don't want to be there at all.)

In other words, an approach that worked when there were few cars became useless with the fantastic and unexpected rise in auto travel. On the other hand, it is tempting to blame the *whole* problem of city congestion on the autuomobile, which would be unfair.

For example, the two views on page 76 of a busy Chicago intersection were made in 1910 and 1966. The apparent un-

Two Views of a Chicago Intersection: 1910 and 1966.

concern of the mounted police officers in the first picture suggests that what looks to us like a major traffic tie-up was not an unusual occurrence. Yet the automobile is nowhere to be seen.

As long ago as the days of ancient Rome, city traffic was a problem. Julius Caesar was forced to ban wheeled vehicles from the center of that city during the day because of congestion.

Even the noise problem associated with transportation is not necessarily worse than it once was. Iron-bound wooden wheels bouncing on cobblestone streets assailed one's ears no less than one's insides.

While opinion varies as to whether conditions are worse now than they used to be, all agree they are bad enough for something to be done. A point worth noting is that worldwide production of motor vehicles is increasing three times faster than the increase in human population. In the United States, highway travel increased 56 per cent in the decade ending 1970, and continues to go up four or five per cent a year. So things are bound to get worse unless something *is* done.

Modern technology has been, and is being, applied to the problems, and solutions are appearing. Clearly, the overall problem is large enough and complex enough that no one solution, such as better transit systems, can be expected to do the job.

Among the measures that have been proposed or are being tried are staggered working hours—having the work day begin at varying times from, let's say, 8 to 9:30 or even 10 A.M.; systematic car pooling; changing the work week to nine hour days or even three 12-hour days; special gasoline and parking taxes; pollutant emissions taxes; establishment of car-free zones in cities; and, finally, a two-car approach involving a low-emission vehicle for cities, and a cheaper,

77

higher emission vehicle for areas where air pollution is not (yet) a problem.

Bypassing the City

One very successful approach has been to simply bypass the problem; that is, to put an *expressway* around or alongside the city. The New Jersey Turnpike, a major link in the New York–Washington trip, simply bypasses Newark and Trenton along the way. Indeed, a driver can travel the full turnpike distance without being stopped by a single traffic light.

For travel in and around the individual city, a slightly different approach is taken. While the shortest distance between opposite edges of a city may be a straight line, where traffic is concerned the shortest trip may well be a curved one.

For example, one can now swing around Baltimore on a fine new Beltway that encircles the city. A number of other cities (among them, Washington, Boston, and San Diego) have tried the beltway idea, and with great success; some use, or will use, more than one at varying distances from the CBD. Thus, people who don't want to enter the downtown area don't have to; they can travel around it.

J. J. Cummings of the Motor Vehicle Manufacturers Association maintains, "Every city that has built even a portion of its planned freeway system already has seen a sharp decline in congestion on its surface streets and a marked increase in peak-hour and off-peak travel speeds on both the freeways and the surface streets."

Furthermore, Mr. Cummings points out that freeways, in spite of the higher speed involved, have a safety record three times as good as conventional city streets.

The first freeway worth talking about, the Bronx River Parkway north of New York City, was built more than 45 years ago. Most freeway development, however, has occurred only in the last quarter-century.

Especially important in metropolitan areas, freeways serve two main functions. They provide rapid and convenient accessibility between different parts of the metropolitan region and between regions, and they separate through traffic from local traffic.

The expressway, or freeway, is a road specially designed to move large volumes of traffic safely at high speeds. The biggest difference between the freeway and the normal street is the controlled-access feature of the freeway.

Specially designed ramps permit traffic to enter and leave the road only at designated points. So-called "acceleration lanes" give entering cars a chance to get up speed so that they can merge with the moving traffic easily and safely. Cars leaving the freeway have special lanes that enable them to slow down gradually before turning off. Over- and underpasses eliminate intersections, one of the worst traffic hazards. Median strips divide opposing lanes of traffic. Pedestrians and parking are barred.

Unfortunately, the idyllic picture we have painted does not hold everywhere. One example is the 50-mile Long Island Expressway running out of New York City. It has scornfully (and with justification) been called "the world's longest parking lot."

A number of suggestions have been made to alleviate the situation. Among them are: building a monorail or express bus lane along the present roadway, building another expressway, double-decking the present one, and charging drivers for the privilege of entering the city by car (unless they can prove they need it). Some humorists suggest closing down Long Island.

Automating the Highway

Another possibility for the future is to automate the highway. This exciting development is usually thought of as a matter of convenience for the driver—a way of allowing him to relax while computers and other electronic devices do the work. *Convenience* is certainly one good reason for developing an automated highway. But there are other, even better, inducements.

A second reason is *safety*. Man is a thoroughly unpredictable animal; while that is his strength in some ways, it is a dangerous trait on the highways. He also has a tendency to fall asleep or to allow his attention to wander when tired or bored. While driving can be fun on local country roads, turnpike driving rarely is; the usual objective is simply to get to the destination in the shortest possible time.

The third argument for automation is perhaps a surprising one, for it is tied in with an unexpected cause of congestion on roads. It is not so much the cars that make the trouble; it is the *spaces* between them! For each ten mph of speed, the safe driver leaves a full car-length of distanc between his car and the one in front of him. Using approximate numbers, we can see that, at 20 mph, a 20-foot car uses up 60 feet of highway (20 feet for the car and 40 feet for spacing). Under these conditions, the roadway will (ideally) carry 1,800 cars past a set point per hour.

At 60 mph, each car requires a block 140 feet long. But because the cars are traveling faster, more will pass the set point in unit time and the highway capacity rises—theoretically. However, slow drivers, lane-changers, and other "troublemakers" keep the figure somewhere between 1,500 and 2,000 cars per hour.

Thus, we can increase the capacity of the roadway in two ways: increase the speed of the cars, and decrease the spacing. With man at the wheel, neither solution is a wise one. With electronics, both are possible.

A few years ago, a continuous guidance cable was buried in an oval track in southern New Jersey. Additional electronic equipment was placed as needed. On the road were two cars equipped with special controls and passengers, but no drivers.

The cars were steered, accelerated, and braked automatically. The passengers were informed of "hazards" and mythical intersections via the car radio. The information came from the guidance cable.

With automatic control, spacing can be cut down considerably, immediately doubling or tripling the capacity of the road. Even in so simple a matter as braking in an emergency, machines not only don't fall asleep, but they also react much faster than humans. It takes an alert driver about a second before he or she even begins to apply the brake after seeing trouble. At 60 mph, the car will travel 88 feet before the brakes even begin to work. A great deal can happen in 88 feet.

It is no surprise that multiple rear-end collisions are a frequent occurrence. One such accident actually involved 200 cars, when drivers on a turnpike apparently misjudged visibility and maintained too close a headway! Machines can apply the brakes immediately.

Even so, will motorists allow control of their cars to be taken away from them? They may well balk at first. Some proposals, therefore, include a "stepped" plan. L. E. Flory of Radio Corporation of America, who was involved in the automatic highway development just discussed, suggests the following set of steps:

1) Better ways of informing drivers, so they can make better and faster decisions.

2) An over-ride system, whereby the equipment takes over

"AUTOLINE"--- *Automatic Highway Concept*

1 A motorist traveling in a normal lane but wanting to enter the Autoline lane would move into the transition lane and signal his desire to enter the Autoline.

2 By putting his car on automatic control, his speed and position would be monitored and adjusted.

3 The car would be automatically guided into posi-

tion at the end of the first available group on the Autoline lane.

4 To leave the Autoline lane, the motorist would first signal his intention to the system.

5 His car would move automatically into the transition lane at the first safe opportunity.

6 He would return his car to manual control and then move into a normal lane.

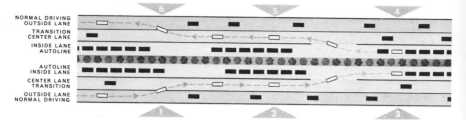

General Motors' Automated "Autoline."

if the driver does not respond to warnings or an emergency situation in time.

3) A completely automated control system.

The roadway might eventually look like that shown here. The outer lanes in each direction are normal, non-automated lanes. The middle lanes in each direction serve for both passing and transition, if desired, to automatic control. At specified points, the driver would signal the system that he wishes to enter. It might be possible at this point for a quick, automatic check to be made of the condition of the vehicle, similar to that now done on spacecraft before blast-off.

Assuming all is well, control would then be taken over by the system and the vehicle would be guided into the first available empty space in the inner lane. Here cars are spaced evenly, but relatively close together. Cruising speed, based on weather, road conditions, traffic density, etc., would be maintained by a central controller. To get off the roadway, the driver would reverse the procedure.

General Motors estimates that groups of vehicles could cruise safely at 70 mph on this Autoline, giving a capacity of 9,000 vehicles per hour—the equivalent of six normal lanes of traffic. Grouping of cars would increase the capacity of the system and save "handling" by the computer. GM also suggests an automated system they call the Metro Guideway that would include captive rapid transit vehicles. These would provide rapid transportation to and from, and within, major activity areas such as downtown sections, airports, universities, and the like.

Some transportation experts see the beginning of automated systems in use within the next two to 15 years, in spite of the fact that it might add as much as $500 to the cost of a car. This sounds at first as if it would put the whole idea out of range. Yet increasing numbers of drivers have been willing to shell out similar amounts for automatic transmission, power steering, and air conditioning.

There is another point that brings automation of roads closer to reality. When completed, the interstate system will make up just over one per cent of the nation's total highway system, but it will be carrying 20 per cent of the total traffic! Clearly automation of even a few selected highways can have a large effect on the highway traffic picture. Other experts feel that fully automated expressways are at least twenty-five years away.

Let us see what kind of developments we can expect in the meantime. One is a possible gradual rise in speeds along the major expressways.

Calspan Corporation (formerly Cornell Aeronautical Laboratory), which is actively engaged in transportation studies, has proposed the *Century Expressway*, a non-automatic highway that would be capable of accommodating cruising speeds of 100 mph or more. A second phase, looking toward speeds of about 150 mph, would require some form of guideway/

vehicle combination that does not depend upon the friction of tires on pavement for maintaining stability and control.

Perhaps one or more of the techniques we have already discussed for guiding trains, such as fluid or magnetic systems, will be used. In any case, it seems clear that such an expressway would be available only to a special class of drivers with a special class of vehicles. Possibly both driver and vehicle would be tested before entry was permitted.

Certainly, careful monitoring of the highway would be required. Modern developments in electronics and computers will make this relatively easy. Experiments are already being carried out on control of expressways based on *television monitoring*.

In Detroit, for instance, the flow of traffic is surveyed continuously by fourteen television cameras spaced at quarter-mile intervals. When a "critical density" of traffic has built up, entrance ramps to the particular section are closed! Traffic is diverted to local roads, or through alternate routes to the next open ramp. This may be a little rough on a few drivers, but on balance, all drivers benefit. A recent study by Michigan State University showed that average speed has increased from 27 to 37 mph, traffic volume has *increased* five to ten per cent, and traffic tie-ups have been cut considerably.

On Chicago's Congress Street Expressway, the intermediate television step is bypassed completely. Monitoring is done entirely with *electronic sensors*. The results are fed into a computer that closes ramps automatically by activating signals directing traffic to other routes. Obviously, such monitoring techniques could be applied for high-speed routes as well. Computerization of traffic lights, in conjunction with sensors that monitor traffic density, has proved its worth in several areas.

Providing the driver with the information needed for intelligent driving and navigating is another area where we can expect some improvement. There is no technical reason why drivers cannot be warned somehow of impending danger, congestion, or other conditions ahead, so that they can take appropriate action early enough to avoid the difficulty. Some roads already have warning signs which indicate ice, fog, or other general conditions.

This could be carried much further. It might be possible, for example, to provide remotely controlled lane indicators, so that drivers do not come upon stopped vehicles so suddenly and unexpectedly that they cannot do anything about it.

In addition to these obvious advantages, a flexible sign system might be useful in other ways. For example, in order to control and meter efficiently the merging of vehicles on high-speed roads and thereby obtain higher capacity, it is necessary to utilize gaps in the main stream as they occur. The heart of such a system is a *gap-measuring device and computer*—both of which are already available.

In effect, the holes in the traffic stream are measured and their speed computed. A vehicle entering a ramp can then be given instructions as to the speed that must be attained in order to meet the gap when it arrives at the merging point. This is very important at high speeds.

The signals to the ramp vehicle will, at least initially, be variable signs that will provide start, speed, and merge information at the appropriate times. The basic logic for the development of this system has already been completed and the development of hardware (actual computer equipment) begun. Experiments on Houston's Gulf Freeway showed great promise for the system.

Once a vehicle is traveling at high speed, however, there is a very strict limit to how much information can be supplied to the driver by signs. This is particularly true at night, or during a long trip when drivers are typically less alert.

Some drivers tend to ignore road signs altogether. Perhaps some sort of variations in the road surface could "speak" the message as the tires roll over them. There is also the possibility of developing a system of communications that would link the driver's radio with recorded or spoken messages wherever needed. A system called DAIR (Driver Aids Information and Routing) was well received by motorists during an experimental run on the Lodge Freeway in Detroit. DAIR also offers two-way communications, so that the driver can radio for aid in case of trouble.

Another exciting area of development is in the vehicle itself. Here are some of the developments that lie in store:

• Control of the car may be lodged in a single control. Perhaps a single "joystick" would provide acceleration when pushed forward, braking when pulled back, and lateral control by turning it left or right. This single-control approach could make it easier to fit the car into an automated system.

• Lighter, stronger materials could make the vehicle lighter. Less power would be required, resulting in fuel savings, and braking could be more efficient for a given size of brake.

• Cars should be easier to fix; perhaps crushable material could be used that would return to its proper shape when heated, cooled, irradiated, or whatever.

• How about a laser-aided viewing system that will see through fog and blizzard, and will display the scene ahead on a TV screen? One has actually been designed.

• Size and cost of computers keep coming down, and we shall surely be seeing much more use of them in the automotive field, which of course includes trucks and buses. They are already being used in the design of vehicles and roadways. Goodrich has developed a computerized skid-control system for trucks, buses, and trailers. We have already seen automatic headlight dimmers, electronic fuel injection, automatic temperature control, and automatic speed control. The next step might be an auto radar system that will either provide warning if the distance to the car in front becomes too small for a given speed, or will actuate the brakes automatically. And Volkswagen has introduced a single plug-in for checking out a variety of systems in the car.

• As shown in the photo, roadside computerized logic systems can be teamed with electronic communications to provide automatic routing instructions at intersections throughout the country.

• Safety has become an important factor. Cars will almost surely provide greater protection during crashes, plus break-

Experimental Route Guidance System combines two-way road-to-vehicle communications with roadside computerized logic.

away steering columns. Some form of passive safety device —one that does not require an action on the part of the driver or passenger to activate it, unlike present-day seat belts—will probably come into use. The experimental air bag may be the answer, but it requires more work to make it foolproof—and better public relations to make it acceptable to the average driver.

A final category of improvement has to do with improved methods for more rapid and efficient removal of obstructions, such as accidents and stalled vehicles, from the roadway. Often, the roadway blocks up so rapidly behind the problem area that a tow truck must crawl along at a snail's pace to get to the spot. Sometimes it must even approach from the opposite direction and then, if there is a median barrier, find some way to cross it.

One approach that has been tried experimentally is to use a helicopter to move or remove the obstruction. While there is no doubt that this works, it is an expensive approach that has not yet been adopted as an operational method.

Highway Underground

If, as city planner Constantinos Doxiados says, all metropolitan surface transportation must eventually go underground, this problem may be solved more easily. George A. Hoffman, of the University of California, has proposed a system of deep tunnels and parking areas as a solution to the present and future ills of the city. Traffic would be carried through tunnels dug by means of the modern techniques we have already discussed. At the same time, there would be overhead, electrified rails on which police and aid vehicles could travel at high speed above jammed lanes. Electrically driven capsules, containing patrolmen well-versed in first aid and fully equipped with ladders, grappling apparatus, and medical supplies, would quickly reach a disabled vehicle, render any medical assistance required, and lift or tow the vehicle out of the way by means of a telescoping crane. A vast system of underground parking spaces is also proposed as an answer to the city parking problem.

Of course, on the scale envisioned by Hoffman, fumes emitted by the passage of thousands of vehicles in an enclosed space would present a terrible hazard to drivers. Yet he feels that the problem is by no means insurmountable. He even suggests that an enterprising company might be able to tap the system's exhaust stacks. Thus, at one stroke, the gases injected into the atmosphere would be purified, and a substantial amount of unburned hydrocarbons (fuel in gaseous form) could be recovered and sold.

There is still another way to approach the fume problem that exists aboveground as well as below, and that is not to generate any in the first place. We'll talk about that in the next chapter.

6

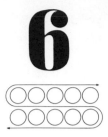

The Electric Car
and the City Center

Even above ground, in the open air, air pollution is now recognized as a serious threat to health, as well as a destructive force to crops and buildings. Automobiles are identified as a major, though not the only, offender. Laws have been passed requiring that measures be taken by automobile manufacturers to cut down on the pollutants emitted in the exhausts of their cars.

Under the Clean Air Act of 1970 cars were required to reduce emissions of hydrocarbons and carbon monoxide by 90 per cent over 1970 amounts in 1975 and nitrogen oxides the same amount by 1976. The car manufacturers were later given an additional year in which to comply with the ruling. To date some progress has been made.

There are several basic approaches that have been taken. The American car manufacturers have so far opted for the standard internal combustion (IC) engine, with equipment added on to prevent the pollutants from entering the atmosphere. This approach clearly has to do with their gigantic investment in the IC engine, along with the fact that it has been brought to a high stage of development.

The added equipment consists mostly of what are called catalytic converters. These use various, and generally expensive, substances (catalysts) to change pollutants such as carbon monoxide and hydrocarbons to harmless water and carbon dioxide, without themselves entering into the chemical reaction.

The equipment, unfortunately, adds several hundred dollars to the basic cost of the car, and the catalysts may have to be replaced every 25,000 to 50,000 miles. Bell Telephone Laboratories, however, is experimenting with a different type of catalyst that, it is hoped, will be cheaper and more reliable.

There are several other problems connected with the use of the catalytic converter approach. Among them are: difficulty in starting and tendency to stall; poorer performance on the road; and poorer fuel economy. In these days of concern with the energy supply, a reduction in gas mileage of six to 11 per cent is considered a very serious drawback.

The more reasonable approach would seem to be some sort of basic change in the engine itself. Of the large number of possibilities in the offing, two come closest to meeting the stringent new air pollution requirements. One engine, now taking the country by storm, is the Wankel or rotary engine. Unlike the conventional piston engine with its rapid vibratory motion, this engine operates strictly on a rotary basis, and hence is less prone to vibration. It also is more powerful per unit size.

Most important, however, is the fact that it does not need a catalytic converter to control unburned hydrocarbon and carbon monoxide emissions. These are reburned in a so-called thermal reactor—actually a simple double-walled muffler. The Mazda, a Japanese import, is currently being sold with rotary engines and is doing very well. One prediction, in Ward's Wankel Report, suggests that by 1980 more than three-quarters of all cars sold in the United States will be rotary-powered.

One problem with the Mazda is that, like the American cars equipped with pollution controls, fuel economy is lower than on non-equipped American cars.

Another Japanese manufacturer claims to have even this problem under control. The Honda Motor Company says its engine, without any additional pollution control devices, can already meet the new emission standards for hydrocarbons and carbon monoxide—without any sacrifice in gas mileage. Company representatives believe the engine can also be made to bring emissions of the third major pollutant, nitrogen oxides, under control as well. The Honda system uses a stratified charge engine combined with a double-chambered carburetor. Most of the troublesome part of the combustion process is handled in one of the chambers rather than in the exhaust system. One advantage is that the design change is less drastic than the rotary type, for the dual-carburetor, stratified charge system is otherwise fitted to a standard piston engine.

There are yet other possibilities in the petroleum-fueled field, such as steam engines and gas turbines. These have not yet been brought to the point of practicality, at least not for cars. (On October 10, 1972, Greyhound Lines put its first turbine-powered bus into regular service.)

But even if one of the engines can meet the rigid government specifiations mentioned earlier, the number of cars and trucks is increasing so rapidly that any progress made is rapidly eaten up by the increasing number of emitters. Almost 95 million cars are now on American roads. If trucks and buses are included, the number jumps to 118 million, or more than one for every two persons.

Many people feel that a more direct approach to the air pollution problem is required. At the moment, the best hope seems to lie in the electric car.

The electric car is not a new idea. The first "practical" electric vehicle was built way back in 1837, fully half a century before the equivalent gasoline-powered car was built. But improvements in the gasoline-powered IC engine were so rapid and so significant that it quickly outstripped the battery as a provider of power. The gasoline-powered car became lighter, more powerful, and could travel considerably longer between service stops. This is still true. A car can make 200–250 miles on one tank of gasoline, while electrics are limited to perhaps 50 miles per battery charge —under good conditions.

As long as there weren't too many cars on the road, these were telling advantages, and the electric car gave way, though it has been around right along. In England, where gasoline is more expensive than it is here, an estimated 80,000 electric vehicles are in use, mainly in the form of delivery vans.

Electric vehicles are used in the United States, too, but mostly in the form of golf carts (which are also being used for street travel in a few areas on the West Coast) and as transporters in large factories. The emission-free operation of electrics explains their use in factories, and the convenent, efficient operation in low-speed, stop-and-go applications makes them ideal for the golf course.

It must be kept in mind that a gasoline engine is burning a considerable amount of fuel even when it is standing still, i.e., when the engine is idling. In the electric car, on the other hand, there is no drain on the battery when the car is stopped. It's like turning off a flashlight.

The Motor Vehicle Manufacturers Association has reported

that 60 per cent of car trips are less than five miles in length (going to the supermarket, the movies, bowling, and so on). And 50 per cent of the use of cars is for going to and from work—with trips avcraging six to ten miles. In addition, half the cars contain only the driver!

Is an 18-foot, 300-horsepower, 2-ton fume-spitter really necessary for this kind of traveling? More and more the answer seems to be, "No."

No one claims that the automobile as we know it today is on the way out, or even that it should be. Certainly, for inter-city and inter-metropolitan driving at 60 to 80 mph along today's marvelous superhighways, and for comfort and convenience, it is a pleasure indeed. Time will bring further refinements, improvements, new designs, even new power plants.

But on the local streets, where more and more cars are fighting for space, where travel is typically at 20 to 25 mph and no more than 30 to 50 miles per day, a different approach is necessary. The small, agile, easily parked electric car certainly seems to be one good answer. Many experimental vehicles have already been built and are running; at least one is even being offered for sale on a trial basis.

Of course, electric cars should be easy to charge. It is already possible to charge them by plugging into a home outlet. Another possibility is metered charging while the car is parked at a meter.

At the moment, almost daily recharging is necessary (depending, of course, on the distances and severity of the driving). Although it is a simple matter, it does take a few hours at least and people are prone to be forgetful. One possibility is to have some kind of automatic recharging whenever the car is driven into a garage or driveway.

In the more distant future, this kind of problem will no longer exist. An experimental vehicle has already been built which can find its way down a corridor by bouncing radio signals off the walls. When batteries need recharging, this experimental vehicle seeks out the nearest electric outlet and plugs in.

If electrics really become popular, many service stations will go out of business. For those of us who have been lucky enough to be near a station when we had car trouble, this will be recognized as a considerable disadvantage. But electrics are much simpler and more reliable. They are less likely to cause trouble, and so the situation may balance out, after all. Service stations may also be able to exchange a set of batteries rapidly, as in the car shown on page 96, and then charge them for the next customer.

On the other hand, the question of convenience may turn out to be quite irrelevant. Research chemist Donald E. Carr maintains that the electric auto is the *only* hope for stopping the otherwise inevitable asphyxiation of our cities.

Since the United States is becoming more and more a two-car-family nation, many families will be able to own at least one electric, as well as a larger and more luxurious gasoline-powered car. But what about people who do not want or cannot afford two cars? Must they buy a large, gasoline-engine car and perhaps eventually be barred from the city altogether? Or must they buy a small electric with its admittedly limited performance?

It is unlikely that this uncomfortable choice will ever have to be made. Ford and GM, for example, are working on a hybrid vehicle that would run on batteries in metropolitan areas and switch to gasoline power when out on the open road. The batteries would automatically be charged when the car was running on gasoline.

Another possibility is a flywheel/gasoline engine hybrid. The flywheel could be spun up at night, or at wayside stations, and would supply clean energy for city driving, with

The "Sundancer" is an 8-horsepower, commuter-type vehicle that uses lead-acid batteries and has a top speed of 60 mph. The bottom photo shows the mechanical components; the batteries can be slid out of the long box for rapid exchange.

the gasoline engine taking over in open areas, or if the flywheel ran down before it could be "recharged."

It is more likely, however, that the vast range of experiment and experience in the battery-driven motor and appliance field (e.g., razors, toothbrushes, carving knives, golf carts, etc.) will lead to electric sources that can provide the performance we expect from present-day cars.

New Sources of Power

Various types of battery systems are already under development. *Alkali-metal batteries* are showing promise, and a *silver-zinc battery* has been developed which has five times the energy density of the common lead-acid type, but is far higher in price. A *sodium-sulphur battery* is 15 times more efficient, but must operate at temperatures as high as 900°F, creating a potentially dangerous situation.

It may one day be possible to develop a *nuclear-powered* car. Not only would such a vehicle be pollution-free, but one pound of uranium can do the job of 360,000 gallons of gasoline! At the moment, however, no one has suggested a way to produce a small, low-cost reactor. Other major problems are the initially high cost of the fuel, the requirements for shielding, and the potential danger of radiation released in a crash.

A more likely candidate, at least at present, is the *fuel cell.* Invented back in the 1800's, this is a device that does not employ the discharge-recharge system batteries require. Instead, it can convert fuel directly and continuously into electricity as long as the fuel is available.

In one form, the fuel cell uses hydrogen and oxygen to provide electricity (and water). General Electric developed this type of system for use in the Gemini space flights. Fuel cells also provided 3,000 watts of electricity for the Apollo Command Module, along with 17 quarts of drinkable water each day.

Unfortunately, the fuel cell is so complex and the fuel so

97

expensive that the system is still far out of the range of the average motorist. However, the Army has tested a 3/4-ton electric truck powered by a 40,000 watt hydrazine-air fuel cell. Results indicate that the truck performs as well as, or better than, a standard 3/4-ton vehicle powered by a 94-hp internal combustion engine. Army engineers believe that a hydrocarbon fuel, which may give *100 to 150 miles per gallon,* can eventually be used to power the fuel cells.

Another possibility is the use of hydrogen and oxygen in a different way. A common chemical experiment splits water into its component hydrogen and oxygen by means of an electric current and then "explodes" these gases back into water. Is it possible that this explosion could provide a simpler system than the fuel cell for propelling a fume-free car?

One of the most exciting aspects of the fuel cell is its remarkably high efficiency—theoretically almost 100 per cent. Practical fuel cells have already been operated at 75 per cent efficiency, which is three times as high as an internal combustion engine. This outstanding ability to convert chemical energy directly into electricity, rather than having to go through a burning or combustion cycle, explains why fuel cells have already been the subject of so much research and development.

Hydrogen gas has also been suggested for use directly as a fuel. Automobile and other engines can be modified to burn this gas with almost zero pollution, though there are complications with storing it. Experiments are also being conducted on the burning of natural gas. Though not as clean-burning as hydrogen, natural gas is still far better in this sense than gasoline. Such experiments may bring closer the day of the "hydrogen economy," in which nuclear, solar, or other energy is used to split water into oxygen and hydrogen, thus providing a virtually unlimited fuel supply.

This standard gasoline-powered car was modified to burn hydrogen. It has a range of about 200 miles at 50 mph.

The electric car approach still seems the more likely outcome, however. We might see it arrive in three more or less separate stages. The first generation of such vehicles might be rented from firms that would own and service them. The second generation would be an improved version, with a high-enough performance level to begin to attract private ownership on a large scale. The third step might be high-performance vehicles powered by batteries.

If this does take place, our air pollution problem will be helped considerably, but it won't be solved. The electricity must still be generated somewhere, somehow. Thus far every form of electrical generating plant has some negative environmental effect.*

And what about the problem of congestion? Will all cars have to be parked outside the city limits the way Japanese leave their shoes outside the house?

* See *Energy in the World of the Future,* another book in this series, for more on this subject.

One answer, as we have seen, is to put everything (except pedestrians) underground. Another is to stick with Phase I of the forecast given above. Perhaps each suburban family will be equipped with a private car, plus a small electric vehicle owned by a regional transportation authority. The commuter, on his way to work, would deliver the car to an office of the authority at his local transit station. That car might be used by several other people during the day, in which case he would simply pick up another car at night to drive home.

Or we might see just the reverse. That is, urban and suburban families would own the smaller electric runabouts, and would rent the larger, more powerful cars (perhaps even electric ones) for the few long trips made during the year.

Widespread use of electric cars would make possible whole new systems of transportation. For example, many routes could be enclosed, providing all-weather comfort and convenience. Developments in *photochromic* glass and plastic would enable transporterways to darken automatically in strong sunlight, thus giving protection against the sun's glare and perhaps heat. Ways might even be found to utilize the heat absorbed by the darkened material, converting it to electricity, for example.

New Means of Mobility

Are cars, even electric runabouts, the only answer to greater mobility in and around the city? How about the approach shown on page 102?

As you can see, the *jet-belt* or, as the Bell Aerosystems people call it, the Pogo, is already a reality. Both one- and two-man devices have been successfully flown many times, at speeds up to 60 mph. With one of these parked in your

An enclosed, all-weather highway.

Bell's "Pogo" Jet-Belt.

The Benson Gyrocopter.

back yard, a trip to the city would be a cinch. And once there, the "vehicle" takes up little enough room. The trip would be a little cold and perhaps wet in the winter, but electrically heated, waterproof clothing could take care of that.

One problem might be that of obtaining fuel, at least at first. Imagine going up to your favorite service station and asking him to "fill-er-up" with nitrogen tetroxide and a 50/50 blend of hydrazine and unsymmetrical dimethylhydrazine—the same fuel that is used for the Apollo lunar module.

Indeed, the Pogo has been proposed for use on the moon, where it would be very useful. Fueling the Pogo might be even easier there than at your service station, for hopefully there would be some fuel left in the lunar module tanks.

A range of about 12 miles is seen for the moon application. On earth, with its much higher gravity, this figure is far lower (less than 1,000 feet). Hence the device, so far, is of much greater interest to the military and space establishments than to the average citizen. Still, there is little doubt that the future will see such devices in use by at least the braver (and richer) among us.

Or how about the long-dreamed-of *personal helicopter?* The cheapest helicopter today runs a smart $25,000, and running and maintenance costs are proportionately high. Of course, as more and more helicopters are manufactured, and with new developments which we take up in Chapter Nine, these costs will undoubtedly come down.

If you don't happen to have $25,000 lying around, but can scrape up 300 feet of clear space for landing and taking off, perhaps the craft shown on the facing page is a better idea. For just under a thousand dollars, plus some do-it-yourself effort, the Benson Gyrocopter should provide a convenient and exciting form of travel. As a matter of fact, if there is a good wind up, you don't even need the 300 feet of space.

103

For the less hardy, improving rail or even road travel is a better answer. In the Bowling Green-Bleecker Street line that ran along Broadway in 1825 (Chapter Two), passengers "stopped" the carriage by yanking a cord attached to the driver's leg. Recent developments in electricity and electronics have provided us with somewhat more sophisticated methods for communication between conveyance and passenger. Elevator passengers need only know how to read numbers and push buttons. With certain refinements, this technique could be applied to horizontal travel as well.

For example, it is quite likely that small electric buses, running on frequent schedules, could provide convenient service even in a car-free CBD. Combining this with the principle of the automatic roadway, we have an automatic, track-free "people mover."

The vehicle could be programmed to stop at passengers' commands—from inside by pulling a cord or pushing a button, and from the stations by inserting a coin or token into a signaling device. Or the system might be a free service of the city or business section, in which case it would only be necessary to press a button at the station. In any case, the number of coins, credit cards, or button pushes could be transmitted to a central dispatch point and used for a flexible schedule that would almost guarantee you a seat.

There would, of course, still be a problem of cross traffic (unless the lines were elevated or depressed, in which case we get involved with the additional bother of stairs or escalators). But this is not an impassible barrier even now, particularly in non-congested, bus-only areas. Automatic transporters, called Robotugs, have already been built which follow tapes along the floor of factories. They can be, and have been, programmed to stop and wait for any cross traffic that does occur.

Already in use in several cities is the *Speedwalk passenger conveyor,* which was widely used at the 1964–65 New York World's Fair. At the San Francisco International Airport, two 450-foot-long Speedwalks (rather like horizontal escalators without steps) are taking some of the walking out of flying. Designed to accommodate 7,200 passengers per hour, they link the United Air Lines ticketing area with the airline's flight gate positions.

One problem with moving sidewalks is that they are slow; they *must* be, in order for passengers to get on and off a steadily moving mechanism safely and easily. Trips of any consequence, therefore, would take an inordinately long time.

In our Prologue, Andrew Mann used an intermediate belt. You will recall that when he got off the "glidewalk," he stepped from the moving belt onto a slower one and then finally onto solid ground. Clearly, a series of these belts can be provided so that, by stepping from one to another, almost any final speed can be obtained.

There is a catch, however. A belt safely moving at 240 feet per minute has a speed just over 2.7 mph. This is still slower than a person can walk. In one lovely science-fiction story, "The Roads Must Roll" by Robert Heinlein, the entire transportation system depended on moving roads, the fastest of which traveled at 100 mph. Mr. Heinlein chose to ignore the fact that some 35 belts running side by side would have been necessary to get the passenger up to that speed.

A most intriguing proposal has recently been made which might be able to overcome this difficult interfacing problem. The Bouladon Integrator starts off as a wide multiple escalator. Dividers separate the wide steps into four or five compartments holding two passengers each, and provide hand-holds as well. The escalator moves forward as usual, but also begins to accelerate sideways. Forward motion of each tier of steps stops as the tiers drop into place one behind the other, thus forming a steadily moving glideway.

105

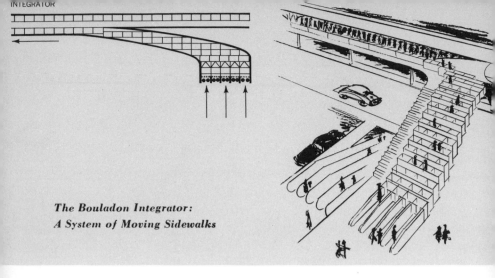

The Bouladon Integrator:
A System of Moving Sidewalks

Speeds of 20 mph or more seem perfectly feasible. The procedure is reversed at the destination.

For a series of stations, the compartment door can be opened onto a train or belt, moving parallel to it and at the same speed, during the "high speed" portion of the run. The escalator, once emptied, then reverses the procedure at the next local stop; it drops off any passengers and starts the run once again.

Clearly, this is a complex and costly affair. For high density areas, however, the continuous service offered would certainly be superior to anything we have now.

I would propose a less complicated arrangement. As shown in the illustration on pages 108 & 109, the job of getting a non-moving passenger onto a fairly rapidly moving belt is given to gravity. When loaded with from one to four people, the unpowered capsule or pallet simply slides down a wheeled, air-cushioned or maglev trackway. At the bottom of, say, a 16-foot drop, it will have reached a speed of some 20 mph, at which point it slides off onto a belt moving at that speed. A slight thump should be all the passengers feel, and the pallet then rests on the belt, which means that no

106

more power need be expended to keep it suspended until it comes time to exit. At that point the speed and momentum of the capsule should, theoretically, be enough to carry it back up a similar slide to the surface. Of course, frictional losses will prevent this, so a powered hook will probably be needed at the exit to be sure the pallet makes it back up to the surface. In any case, no braking is needed; at the stations, relatively simple "turnarounds" can be used to send the vehicle back in the other direction or ahead to the next station if that is where the next passenger wants to go. The capsules, being simple, are inexpensive so that many can be purchased, permitting frequent service. Alternatively, a grid system can be put together, using the turnarounds at the stations for connections. Air jets, linear motors, or powered wheels in the turnaround can be used to control direction of the capsule.

A multi-station system can also be created by raising the "capsule catcher" out of the way. At this point, however, the simplicity of the system is lost; other approaches begin to look more attractive.

Indeed, at this point we find ourselves in the middle of one of the most exciting developments in transportation. This is personal rapid transit (PRT) as opposed to mass or bulk transit. Until now, mass transit has meant just that—the individual traveler has been at the mercy of the average traveler. That is, an "average" destination was chosen, which was sort of in the middle of an area, and a central station was placed there. A rider then had to walk, take a cab, or be picked up to complete his trip. If he has taken an "express" he is pretty sure to need some other form of transportation at the stop in order to complete his trip, i.e., another train (the "local"), a cab, or a bus. If he is on a local, or on a bus, he has to suffer through a "million" other stops where other passengers are picked up or discharged. Indeed,

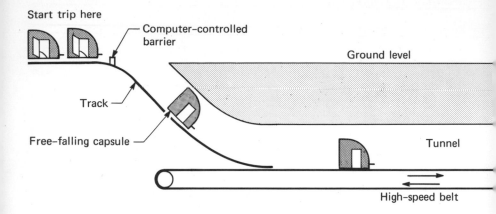

Start trip here

Computer-controlled barrier

Ground level

Track

Free-falling capsule

Tunnel

High-speed belt

A Gravitationally Accelerated an[

for the typical traveler, as much as three-fifths of his time is taken up by loading and unloading, traffic stops, and walking to and from stops.

Modern technology is making possible individual rapid transit with vehicles programmed, or at least cued, by the traveler, to go directly to his stop, bypassing all others along the way. Although travel along exclusive rights-of-way adds to cost and land use, it also permits higher speeds and safety than the bus-type electric people movers we mentioned earlier. Before we describe PRTs, however, some clarification of terminology is probably necessary.

As we saw earlier, systems like those in Morgantown and the two airport systems have been labeled PRTs. I would have been happier if that term had been reserved for the type of system we are describing here, one that is truly personal—in other words, a system in which each small car is used only by persons traveling together.

108

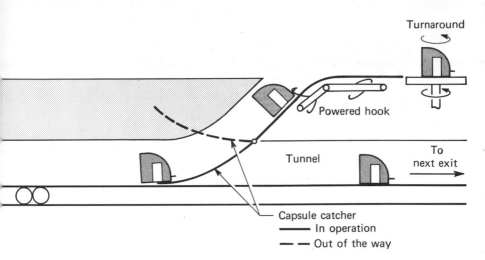

Turnaround

Powered hook

Tunnel

To next exit

Capsule catcher
——— In operation
— — Out of the way

Braked Urban Transit System

A true PRT system will have many stations, from which one can choose one's destination. Anyone can travel alone if he wishes—and directly to his destination. Ideally there will be enough cars available so that one need never wait. While unlikely, this could be the case because the same cars are used over and over again; they do not simply sit and take up space once they have done their job, as automobiles do. All calls for cars will probably be routed to a central control, which continually monitors the system. This control will consider the traffic balance and shunt unused cars to stations where and as they are needed.

There is a great deal of interest being shown in these systems, one of which is illustrated on page 110. And well there might be. Professor J. Edward Anderson of the University of Minnesota says, "For the same number of dollars, a PRT system could put ten times as much of an urban area within walking distance of stations as a rapid-rail transit

Model of an elevated Personal Rapid Transit (PRT)
system shown interface with a high rise building at the
mezzanine level.

system." He adds: "Studies have shown that in a typical
city situation one PRT vehicle will replace about ten cars."*

The PRT is not suited for high-speed operation. It will
typically operate at between ten and 50 mph and will be
completely automatic and monitored for safe operation.
If combined with the linear motor and air-cushion or maglev

* "PRT: Urban Transportation of the Future," *The Futurist*, February 1973.

suspension, we would have a system that might indeed lure large numbers of riders out of their automobiles.

Cities reported to be considering PRT (or People Mover) systems in their transportation plans are Atlanta, Dallas, Denver, Honolulu, Las Vegas, Miami, Minneapolis, Pittsburgh, Salt Lake, and Toronto.

Whether such systems will be built and used in CBDs remains to be seen. Until they are, there are simpler, and perhaps unexpected, solutions to the urban travel problem. A few of these are presented in the following chapters.

7

Road/Rail
Systems

My wife and I had been touring Yugoslavia and Greece by car for a month. We had left our two children with my wife's sister who was living in Germany at the time, and were anxious to get back and see them. Our destination was Salzburg, Austria, where we planned to spend the night.

At Spittal, Austria, we had a choice of three routes: 1) 70 miles in one direction over relatively poor, winding mountain roads, 2) 90 miles over somewhat better mountain roads, or 3) 66 miles over fairly good, flat roads.

The third route was made possible by a five-mile tunnel cut through solid rock. Since automobile exhausts would have quickly filled the tunnel to a poisonous level, and air-conditioning would have been a very difficult job in the heart of a mountain, a car-on-train "piggy-back" system is used in the tunnel.

There was little question in our minds. We had already

driven several hours that day and looked forward to getting to Salzburg. We drove the 23 miles to the beginning of the tunnel and pulled into line behind other cars. In a few minutes, the train, not much more than a flat car with guides, pulled into the station. We drove onto the train and relaxed. About ten minutes later, we started off through the tunnel. Ten minutes after that, we emerged on the other side, relaxed and refreshed.

On to Salzburg! Time saved: 1 1/2 hours.

A number of tunnels like this are in use in the more mountainous areas of Europe. While short tunnels can be, and are, used for autos traveling under their own power, longer ones would be very difficult to keep from being contaminated by the engine exhausts. Such railroad/car combination systems may well be prototypes of a development that will become more widespread, and not just in mountainous areas.

For long-distance travel, remaining in the car would be neither convenient nor comfortable. In a recently instituted piggy-back service connecting Alexandria, Virginia (near Washington, D.C.), and Sanford, Florida, passengers ride in one of the passenger lounge cars or a sleeper, though they can leave luggage in their cars. Thirteen autos can be carried on each of the train cars, up to a maximum of 104 cars per train.

The new service, called Auto-Train, has turned out to be one of the few bright spots in rail travel in recent years. The very first advertisement in *The New York Times* brought so many calls that the company's lines were jammed for days.

Rates are $190 per car, which covers the driver and one passenger. Additional passengers are charged $20 apiece. Sleeping accommodations are extra. Included in the price are a supper and movies for adults and children.

The great advantage of the Auto-Train is that the driver can leave the long-distance driving to the railroad—without los-

Loading the upper deck of the Washington, D.C.—Sanford, Florida Auto-Train. Passengers ride in comfort in separate coaches.

ing the convenience of having his own car with him when he arrives. Travelers with young children will perhaps appreciate this most.

Another advantage is that it eliminates the old problem of "interfacing" two or more systems—that is, transferring from auto to train, and then back again to rented auto, taxi, bus, or subway at the other end. A trip I once took from a New Jersey town to Boston required, in addition to a one-hour flight, five other transportation modes and an additional 3 1/4 hours.

The road/rail system takes advantage of the old adage, "If you can't beat 'em, join 'em." In other words, collection and delivery systems (auto, bus, subway, etc.) are combined with the trunk line.

When, and if, the 32-mile Channel tunnel, which would connect England and France, is built, autos will be carried across the English Channel on double-decked railroad cars in 45 minutes. The trip now takes about two hours by ferry and is normally a very rough crossing; almost universal seasickness is one of the major reasons for a long-standing interest in the project.

It looks at the moment as if the Channel tunnel ("chunnel") is finally going to be built—at a cost of more than $500 million! It should be noted, however, that the project has been under discussion for more than two centuries and that digging was actually begun once before, in 1878.

For the more distant future, a strange-looking vehicle has been designed. Spanning two sets of tracks, the RRollway would permit sideways loading, which would be far more rapid and convenient than the end-on, one-after-another systems now in use. Furthermore, the extremely wide gauge (17 1/2 feet from rail to rail) would provide great stability, making 200 mph speeds quite practicable.

Yet a little thought convinces us that even this technique is far from perfection. One big problem is that of intermediate stops. If we travel at 200 mph, the trip from Alexandria to Sanford would take 4 1/2 hours. This is fine, if you happen to be leaving Alexandria or points north.

The late Charles Kettering of General Motors once told this story: He was traveling by car in a backwoods section of Kentucky where there were few roads. It wasn't long before he became lost. A little while later, he overtook a resident of the area and asked him how to get to Cincinnati from there.

"Well," the man said, "you go up here to the fork. There you turn left. Let me see. No, I guess you'd better turn right. Well now, to tell you the truth, if I was goin' to Cincinnati, I just wouldn't start from here."

The point, of course, is that we don't want the motorist in Raleigh, North Carolina, to feel that he just shouldn't have started from there if he wanted to take the new railroad to Florida. So we must have intermediate stops. But then another problem arises: if the train were to make ten stops of even a short three minutes apiece, a total of fifty minutes would be added onto the trip. The extra twenty minutes is taken up in slowing down and accelerating for each stop. Average speed is thereby reduced from 200 mph to 166.

Obviously, this is not a problem which is solely restricted to car-carrying trains. It affects all trunkline carriers, indeed all public transportation. The traditional solution is the use of express and local service, with the usual problems of interfacing them and the necessarily slow pace of the locals.

In-Motion Transfers

A better solution is to effect transfer between train and station without requiring the main train (or other vehicle) to stop. This might very well be the greatest advance we can make in our transportation of the future, for it can work in all areas—in long, medium, and short distance travel. There are several ways of accomplishing this.

One basic approach is illustrated in *Figure A,* page 117. Passenger-carrying "capsules" are exchanged between the through-train and a local which is rapidly brought up to matching speed. The two trains, local and express, are locked together for a few moments, and the capsules are exchanged with dispatch. To the passengers, the initial motion of the local might feel like a fast take-off at a traffic light.

The exchange of passengers is something like handing a ham sandwich from your car window to that of your next-lane neighbor, when and if both speeds could be matched and held. (I don't recommend this, even as a lark. Autos do not have the train's lateral stability, which is provided by the

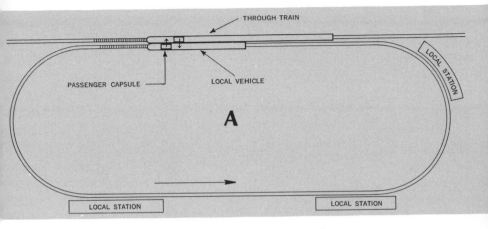

Two passenger-carrying exchange systems.

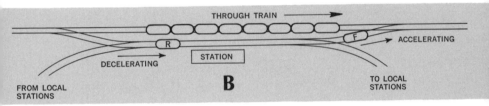

straight rails and flanged wheels. Indeed, precise positioning of trains made possible by this system is one of the reasons why steel wheels are suggested for the gravity-vacuum train.)

An exciting alternative, and one which makes sense when "traffic" is heavier, is to transfer *entire train cars.* The process might start by having one or more train cars (pods) waiting in a station. Passengers get on and are seated. At a certain time, determined by computer, the doors close and the self-propelled pod starts moving. As shown in *Figure B,* the pod (*F*) accelerates rapidly and moves out in front of the fast-moving through-train.

This is similar to the docking maneuvers that take place

117

during rendezvous between a space ship and a speeding capsule in orbit. Even though both craft may be zipping along at 18,000 mph, an astronaut can step from one to the other exactly as if both craft were standing still. The only requirement is that both craft be traveling the same course and at the same rate of speed. In the train system, the "rendezvous" is accomplished with no loss of time or speed for the through-train.

At the same time, as the train is approaching the station, one or more cars (R) are dropped off the rear of the train and are brought to a stop at the local station. The potential of this system is great because the local vehicle can then become part of the local distribution system. If two cars are dropped, one might go in one direction and the second in another.

Rail-Bus Systems

These local vehicles need not be restricted to tracks. They could, for example, be fitted with rubber tires and moved out into a local, flexible, distribution mode. Thus, the same vehicle might travel 200 mph on the trunk line, 70 mph along a computer-controlled route such as the BART line in the San Francisco area, and, finally, pick up a driver (if necessary) and operate as a conventional bus on the streets of a city.

The remarkable flexibility of such a system (here, for the first time, we have the right to use the word "system") can be illustrated by a more localized example. Let us mark one of our railbuses "New York City," and have it take a morning route through Englewood, New Jersey. At the same time, we will have another such vehicle, also marked "New York City," circulating through Hackensack, New Jersey. After collecting passengers in their respective cities, the two vehicles pick up the rarely used Erie tracks heading south. While in motion, they meet and couple. The front bus is then designated "Downtown" or "City Hall" and the rear one is marked "Midtown" or "Grand Central."

When the two railbuses couple (convoy grouping), the doors between them are opened and free movement between them becomes possible. The passengers then regroup themselves. The burden of sorting passengers thus falls on them rather than on the system. (Clearly, this is only feasible on an exclusive right-of-way such as a railroad track, or perhaps a bus-only lane. Unexpected stops for other traffic would be very dangerous.)

At Secaucus, the railbuses uncouple; the front vehicle heads for the Lincoln Tunnel. Once on the New York side, it circulates through the midtown area, preferably on bus-only lanes, making several stops along the way. The other railbus continues south, then moves through the Holland Tunnel and circulates in the City Hall area. Two vehicles have covered areas that would normally require four.

The only questionable feature of this system is the requirement that passengers rearrange themselves while the vehicle is still moving. Of course, this is done constantly on the New York City subways, and for less reason, namely to be closer to an exit or stairway. In truth, it is only dangerous during the lurching starts and stops experienced in the antiquated subway system, and during sharp curves. In a modern system, starts and stops as well as curves could be much smoother. Actually, when the railbus is in steady motion, it is no different from any other train, in which people have been walking and even eating for many years.

Really then, the rearrangement simply amounts to a one-time round of "musical chairs" for some of the passengers; the rest will already be in the right car. In exchange for this, the passengers can enjoy rapid, practically door-to-door transportation.

Naturally, the railbus systems are in the relatively distant future. The first steps already have been taken, however. The Port of New York Authority, in cooperation with the Metropolitan Transportation Authority, has initiated a test program to determine the practicability of a bus-rail vehicle.

Such a vehicle, utilizing retractable steel wheels as well as rubber tires (see photo below), could bypass a large part of the current traffic bottleneck by making part of the run between Manhattan and Kennedy International Airport on existing Long Island Rail Road trackage. It would perform as a regular bus at both ends of the trip.

Results of the testing, however, are not promising. There seemed to be problems with lateral stability, among other things. But the basic idea remains an interesting one.

Railbus with steel wheels and rubber tires.

Rapid Transit Experimental (RTX) Coach. General Motors' entry for a DOT program to develop a "standard 40-foot urban bus" that will be quieter, more comfortable, and easier to get into and out of than current models.

As an alternative to the railbus, the Department of Transportation has asked industry to come up with proposals for some form of a bus that could operate automatically in a guideway, while retaining the capability of being driven on local streets. It remains to be seen whether a practical system can be devised.

Bus Travel

The importance of bus travel should not be minimized, because of all forms of mass transit the bus comes closest to providing door-to-door transportation.

To help speed buses along their way, a number of innovations are being tried, or have already come into use. One is to reserve traffic lanes for buses only. This is being done both for express-type commuter lanes, as in the very successful Shirley Highway project in Virginia, and in local city traffic as well. In Paris the buses operate *against* the traffic flow; this works very well in keeping motorists out of the bus lanes.

Another innovation is bus-controlled traffic lights. Doesn't it seem reasonable that one bus containing 50 people should have priority over 20 cars containing 30 people? As the bus approaches an intersection, a radio signal automatically turns the signal in the bus's favor. To prevent problems where bus routes cross, the traffic light will only "accept" a signal from one direction at a time.

In a pilot project now in operation at Haddonfield, New Jersey, door-to-door transportation is being provided, at least within the five-square-mile selected area which serves about 25,000 people. A telephone call brings a small, radio-dispatched bus to the caller's door within ten to 20 minutes, which will take him anywhere within the area, though perhaps not directly. In essence the Dial-A-Ride vehicle is like a taxi cab which you share with others. It makes sense. Cost, as one would expect, is between bus and cab fare; but more important, it eliminates the need to make changes or the problem of not being able to get to your destination altogether by means of public transport. Service started in 1972, and so far results look very promising. The system is particularly useful to the old, the young, the poor, and the handicapped, and the suburban housewife without a car. It has also proved useful for anyone going to Camden or Philadelphia by train, including, though not importantly as yet, commuters.

Among the advantages are 24-hour, seven-day-a-week service and high security against crime, especially in off hours.

Obviously programming is a complex operation; in the initial phase manual control is being used. If demand warrants it, Dial-A-Ride service will be expanded and computer control instituted.

Track / Auto Systems

Exciting and promising though such bus systems might be, we must face the fact that many people would still prefer to travel in their own cars. As we know, if standard automobiles are used, automating the system is a very difficult problem. But if a guideway system is used, along with electric cars, and if both track and car are designed together as a system, then the problems, though still severe, are minimized somewhat. The electric car can draw both propulsion energy and steering guidance from the guideway.

Several systems have been proposed. One, the Alden StaRRcar (for Self Transit Rail and Road), is shown on page 124. It utilizes its own rubber tires for suspension and propulsion, but is guided along a concrete guideway. While it can be propelled by its own electric motor, it can also be whizzed downtown on a track which would guide, control and power the car. Close headways would be computer-controlled and speeds would be around 60 mph.

At the station, one of several conveniently located in the CBD, the motorist simply gets out of the car. It is then set aside until someone else needs it; perhaps it is dispatched for use elsewhere.

At night, the driver picks up the first available car, travels along the guideway to his local stop, then drives along local streets until he reaches home. He can then keep the car overnight, in which case the charge would be higher than for the simple trip from station to station.

Another possibility, proposed by researchers at Cornell Aeronautical Laboratory (now Calspan Corporation), is the

Alden's StaRRcar.

Urbmobile, which is similar in concept to the StaRRcar. One possible form envisions the Urbmobile traveling like a railroad car as shown here, utilizing flanged steel wheels on steel rails for travel on the guideway, and regular rubber tires for local street travel. The steel wheels would be on the same axles but "inside" the rubber wheels, just as in the bus-rail vehicle shown on page 120.

Preliminary work suggests a vehicle with a top speed of 40 mph on the tires and 60 mph on the guideway. It would have a range of at least 40 miles between each charge, which could be accomplished in the manner described earlier for any electric car, or while the vehicle was traveling along the guideway. Lead-acid batteries are being investigated, along with the more advanced batteries and fuel cells now under development (see Chapter Six).

Calspan's Urbmobile.

The Urbmobile would be 12 to 13 feet long and five feet wide. Unloaded weight would be some 2,000 pounds. (A standard Volkswagen is 12 feet long, five feet wide, and weighs 1,764 pounds.) Small buses and freight vehicles are also being considered.

A normal 12-foot-wide expressway lane carries an average of 3,000 people an hour in rush hours. The small size of the Urbmobile, the close spacing possible, and the guided mode of travel promise movement of as many as 20,000 people per hour along an eight-foot guideway.

In the study, researchers laid out a system on paper with 15 to 25 miles of automatic guideway along the most heavily traveled routes from downtown Buffalo to suburbs north and east of the city, with a spur to the south also. Stations would be spotted about one mile apart in the core, and two to three miles apart farther out. Terminals for automatic storage of Urbmobiles would be located at these points. There will also be parking areas for standard automobiles whose owners might want to use the Urbmobile to get to work.

As with the StaRRcar, the big advantages of the Urbmobile are reduction of air pollution and of congestion, together with door-to-door mobility and convenience. Finally, the system is also thought of as a possible high-speed intercity link.

One of the goals of the Urbmobile study was to determine the best possible combination of guideway and vehicle, and then to compare this with a *pallet type system*. In the latter, the car is driven onto a platform, or "pallet," which is then transported along the guideway. This is similar in principle to the car-on-train systems we mentioned earlier.

For example, seen here is a Westinghouse concept that provides the car-carrying equivalent of a type of People Mover system actually in use in Disneyland, California. As you can see in the second drawing, the operation has been

126

The Westinghouse car-on-train pellet system.

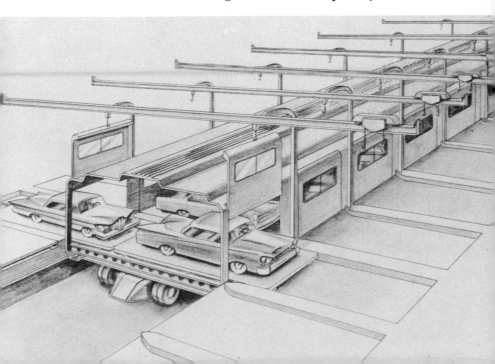

taken out of the hands of the driver once he parks his car on the pad or pallet. Now flat tires or stalled engines cannot hold up the entire operation. Since the motive power for the entire system rests in conventional, highly perfected electric induction motors, reliability of the system should be high. An alternative type of drive could be the LIM, or the electric arc/air-driver system described earlier.

We are, of course, still plagued with the problem of intermediate stops. As usual, someone has made a proposal which takes this into account. Edward N. Hall of United Aircraft proposes mile-long trains which never stop from one end of their run to the other. Pre-loaded shuttle cars accelerate from the station, lock onto the through-train, exchange palletized autos (rather as we did with passenger capsules on page 117), and then dip below the track and finally come to a stop on the other side. There, the procedure is reversed for trains which come from the opposite direction.

It should be pointed out that while the StaRRcar and Urbmobile systems may seem simpler and more desirable than the pallet systems at first glance, there are still serious technical difficulties in implementing them. Suppose a car is derailed for some reason, or loses power.

The long headways on expressways serve a purpose. They allow following cars to be brought to a halt before colliding with the car in trouble. On a train system, or even in a locked-convoy grouping of cars, if a problem arises the whole train simply slows down *as a unit*. People may be thrown out of their seats, it is true; but 200 cars don't go plowing into one another.

There are other approaches to the pallet system as well. Edward J. Ward, chief of the Advanced Systems Division, Federal Railroad Administration, points out that individual pallets would provide some useful advantages. First, the driver would not be at the "mercy" of the train scheduler.

Second, it would not be necessary to modify the standard auto in any way; it would simply be driven on and the brakes set. Third, system reliability would be much higher than it would be if individual's vehicles had to be counted on, for the pallets would be inspected and maintained by the organization on a routine basis.

Mr. Ward foresees speeds up to 150 mph in such a system. He adds that if rubber tires were used, this "could solve a dilemma which has plagued proponents of automated highways for many years—should roadways with the necessary control provisions be constructed first with the hope that the public will purchase automobiles with matching control equipment, or should construction of highways be delayed until sufficient numbers of properly equipped automobiles have been manufactured? Rubber tire Pallets can solve this problem, as the system operator will construct both roadways and vehicles."*

Mr. Ward also indicates how such a pallet system might evolve into an automated highway. The control boxes (for acceleration, braking, etc.) could be designed for installation on private vehicles, and the pallet gauge or tread chosen to match that of a "typical" auto. As more and more autos used the guideway the pallets might be phased out altogether.

Piggy-back, pod, pallet, or individual-vehicle/guideway which shall it be? Most probably, *all* will find use somewhere and sometime in the future.

---

* "Merger of Ground Transportation and Automobiles," *Rail International,* February 1970, p. 76.

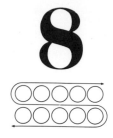

Above and Below the Sea

FOR THOUSANDS of years, wind and wave conspired now and then to make water journeys unbelievably miserable affairs. Only a century and a quarter ago, Charles Dickens wrote of a trip he took to America:

What the agitation of a steam-vessel is, on a bad winter's night in the wild Atlantic, it is impossible for the most vivid imagination to conceive. To say that she is flung down on her side in the waves, with her masts dipping into them, and that, springing up again, she rolls over on the other side, until a heavy sea strikes her with the noise of a hundred great guns, and hurls her back—and that she stops, and staggers, and shivers, as though stunned, and then, with a violent throbbing at her heart, darts onward like a monster goaded into madness, to be beaten down, and battered, and crushed, and leaped on by the angry sea . . . is nothing.

Waves are not only involved in making the ride a rough

one now and then. They are the main reason that conventional ship design is limited to some 35 mph. Surface vessels *create* waves as well as take them. The faster the ship travels, the larger these waves; small-boat enthusiasts have shaken many a fist, at least mentally, at large, fast boats whose waves have threatened to engulf them. The energy that goes into creating these waves, as well as other, less obvious turbulence, can come from only one place: the ship's propulsion mechanism. Such energy is simply subtracted from the energy that can be put into propulsion.

One obvious answer to this problem is to somehow lift the hull up out of the water. One method is commonly called a hydrofoil. When at rest, the hydrofoil craft looks pretty much like any other boat of its size. In fact, the shape of the hull is very similar to any other high-speed boat. The difference lies in the wing-like structures that project below the bottom of the boat's keel. These provide lift to the craft in much the same manner that wings provide lift to an aircraft. At low speeds of 20 mph or less, the craft operates as a conventional boat. As it picks up speed, however, the small foils provide enough lifting force to bring the entire craft right up and out of the water.

At this point there is so much less mass traveling through the water that resistance is cut considerably and speeds can go up. There are hydrofoils in the water today which have speeds up to about 70 mph. Others being developed will have speeds well over 100 mph. John Jones, assistant to the president of North American Aviation, envisions gas-turbine propelled, hydrofoil merchant ships capable of speeds up to 300 mph.

A 40-ton, 75-passenger craft might ride eight to ten feet above the surface of the water, which means that even in quite rough seas the craft would still be riding above the waves.

But submerged foils are only part of the reason why a hydrofoil can cut through rough seas without discomfort to her passengers. Each foil has movable control surfaces tied into an automatic flight-control system similar to those used in jet aircraft. As we know, mechanical and electronic equipment can react much faster than man. As forces are generated by sea and wind which tend to toss the boat around, sensors detect them and "give orders" to the foils which keep the craft on an even keel. Thus, passengers can sit comfortably while the sea thrashes about beneath them.

Hydrofoils have been put into service in a number of areas around the world. There are said to be a thousand in use in the Soviet Union. In the United States several commercial ventures have been tried; most, for various reasons, have ended in failure.

The Boeing Company hopes to reverse this unhappy trend with a new design now in the prototype production stage. This is a large craft by hydrofoil standards—91 feet long, 100 tons, and capable of carrying 250 passengers in a double-deck configuration. There are no propellers. The craft, called Jetfoil, is powered by jet turbine engines driving water pumps. Water is sucked up into the system through either the hull or some of the struts and is jetted out the back of the craft, thus driving it forward. Special controls will give Jetfoil tremendous maneuverability; at slow speeds it can actually pivot around its center.

Jetfoil will cruise at 50 mph, and is expected to provide a smooth ride even over 12-foot waves!

The vertical surfaces of hydrofoils make them very maneuverable at high speeds and reduce the tendency all boats have to side-slip during turns. But hydrofoils have other problems. One is that they require relatively deep channels when they are not "flying." Many, including Jetfoil, are built with retractable foils to get around this problem.

Another difficulty is that of debris in the water. At the slow speeds of conventional marine vessels, logs and other floating hazards are usually pushed aside by the hull. The combination of high speeds and slim supporting struts have made large floating debris a serious problem to hydrofoils.

In the unusual case of an encounter with a large, hard object, hydrofoils are generally designed so that, upon impact, the foils will break off without ripping a hole in the hull, and the vessel settles into the water. Rapid deceleration results, however, with possible injury to passengers. Such problems are not theoretical; a number of commercial hydrofoil operations have foundered because of them. Unfortunately, the only places where there is enough business around to support a commercial hydrofoil operation are just those places where the water is likely to be clogged with debris.

Artist's concept of "Jetfoil," Boeing's large hydrofoil craft.

The Hydro-Ski may provide one answer to these problems. It has no appendages that ride in the water. Rather, the three-hulled device rides above the water, with less and less of it in the water as the speed builds up. This is accomplished by changing the angle of the outside hulls or pontoons as the speed builds up. Eventually the Hydro-Ski craft is being supported only on the rear portions of the outside hulls.

Theodore Davi, president of Hydro-Ski of New Jersey, Inc., claims Hydro-Ski will give a smoother ride than hydrofoils, and that it will ride over debris without damage or passenger discomfort. The first proposed run would be from Keyport on the New Jersey shore to the Wall Street area of Manhattan.

While hydrofoil and Hydro-Ski craft will continue to be used along and across rivers and on coastal runs, it is unlikely that they will be used for transportation purposes along deep-sea routes, even with more development. Research has indicated that the largest practical displacement for these craft ranges somewhere between 500 to 2,000 tons. This is quite small by current ocean-going standards. The giant *Queen Mary*, now retired from service, weighed about 80,000 tons. More typical ocean liners range in the 20,000–30,000 ton class.

Unlike the hydrofoils, the surface effect ship (SES)—a variation of the air-cushion vehicles we have already discussed—becomes *more* efficient as the size increases. That is, it takes less power per pound to drive a 10,000 SES than it does a 5,000 tonner. Both military and civilian planners, eager to shatter the speed limits imposed by conventional large-ship design, see some rather fantastic things in store.

Like the hydrofoil the SES flies, but in a different manner. Its name, "surface effect ship," is derived from the fact that it operates several feet above the surface of the water, supported solely on a cushion of air.

Artist's concept of a Surface Effect Ship (SES).

There are two major ways of supplying this cushion. One is aerodynamically, wherein air moving by at high speeds acts on airfoil surfaces to provide lift. Two designs are possible. In the Weiland airfoil type, actual wing-like structures are used. In the channel-flow type, the underside of the craft itself acts as the airfoil.

For various technical reasons, the aerodynamic type has been more or less bypassed (so far) in favor of the second major type, the aerostatic lift vehicle. This type is also called the air cushion vehicle, or ACV (see Chapter Three). Here the craft forces enough air down through its bottom surface to maintain a cushion of air between it and the surface below.

As with the air-cushion train, pressure must be maintained under the craft by the continuous addition of new air to replace the air leaking out from the back, front, and sides of the craft. Typically, the SES is also propelled forward by the use of separate aircraft-type propellers, although other methods of propulsion, such as waterjets, are being evaulated. A speed of 150 mph is considered well within the realm of the SES.

One way to increase the over-all efficiency of this type of craft is to surround the air with some form of enclosure, in order to cut down on leakage. The result is a "captured air bubble." For example, Booz, Allen Applied Research, Inc., designed a vessel of this type for the U.S. Department of Commerce. In this craft, projected at about 1,000 tons, the sides are dropped into the water. At the same time, a flexible set of "skis" is attached to a curtain at the front and rear. These ride the water to adjust for the rise and fall of the sea as the craft speeds along. Design data have also been provided by Booz, Allen for vessels up to 10,000 tons.

Future-oriented thinkers in the Navy can see an SES as big as an aircraft carrier reaching a speed of 90 mph in a few minutes and eventually reaching a top speed of perhaps 140 to 150 mph. Such a ship could cross the Atlantic in less than a day, or one-fifth the time required by the fastest liner in service today.

While ships of this size remain projections for the future, a number of smaller ACVs have been built and are now in service. Great Britain is represented by the world's largest ACV, the 168-ton Seaspeed. Shown on page 137, the vessel can shuttle some 600 passengers across the English Channel in 30 minutes at speeds of up to 75 mph. Alternatively, it can carry about 30 autos and up to 250 people.

The most advanced of the United States craft is the Navy's still experimental SES-100B. This 100-ton vessel attained a speed of more than 80 mph on March 1, 1973. Bell Aerospace, the designer and builder of the craft, was awarded a $2.9-million contract to conduct a preliminary design study for a 2,000-ton operational prototype SES.

British Rail's Seaspeed.

On March 1, 1973, this SES-100B test craft obtained a speed of over 70 knots.

A major advantage of the SES over the hydrofoil, for certain applications at lesst, is its capability of riding over the surface of the water without touching it. It can therefore travel across ice and debris and even up onto land, with no trouble at all. Think of what this would mean to inhabitants of such places as Pelee Island, in Ontario, Canada, who are quite isolated from both the Canadian and American mainlands after the winter ice has formed on Lake Erie.

Due to the nature of the vessels, ACVs are often called "hovercraft." Since they are not limited to water, they are sometimes also called GEMS, or *ground effect machines.*

Large-scale development of ACVs along these lines could even cause important changes in economic and political situations. Coastal cities, now extremely important because of their proximity to water (though no longer as important as they were before the development of railroads, trucks, and aircraft), might see a further decline in relative importance.

However, it is unlikely that coastal cities such as Boston, New York, and San Francisco will be deserted in the next few years. ACVs are certainly not the complete answer to all the problems besetting shippers and travelers—no one service can be—and a number of serious problems remain to be solved.

Unless the hovercraft is operating in virtual wilderness, travel at high speed in fog or darkness can be extremely hazardous. In and around coastal waters and on rivers, however, travel at high speed is dangerous even under good conditions. Boats, in general, are less maneuverable than landcraft, especially at higher speeds; without contact with solid matter, they tend to skid during turns. Obviously, hovercraft are even more subject to this problem.

This is one of the reasons I have chosen to discuss ACVs in the chapter on watercraft. They could, obviously, be grouped with landcraft as well. We have all read or heard of

A Voyageur Air Cushion Vehicle unloading its cargo of oil drums in the Arctic. The icelocked ships in the background have to wait out the winter and early spring.

the car of the future which will be supported by pads or cushions of air. This sounds fine, but unless exclusive rights-of-way are provided, I would hate to be around when the first one tries to maneuver in traffic.

For those who might be interested, let me repeat Newton's second law of motion: *A body in motion tends to remain in motion, and will continue moving in the same direction, unless acted upon by some external force.* In cars, that force is the friction of tire on pavement—for both stopping and turning. In the typical ship, the force is a combination of water resistance, water against rudder, and perhaps reversal of propellers. The same techniques can be used for air but are far less effective. It is for this reason that the only land-craft seriously being considered along these directions are the air-supported trains we have already discussed.

Cargo Carriers

Thus far we have concentrated on speed. Another trend that shows no sign of becoming unpopular is one toward size, in tankers anyway. Freighters have already been designed and built to carry 3,500 automobiles! But the real giants are the tankers, particularly oil carriers. At this point, 200,000-tonners are fairly common (though too large to be handled at any of our ports), while a 500,000-tonner is being built, and a one-million-tonner is planned to be built in the late seventies. These massive supertankers call for a whole new set of port facilities and requirements. Some, in spite of their great size, are so highly automated that they need as few as nine men to operate them.

Another innovation, introduced in 1971, is the use of barges which can be loaded at local ports and then lifted right onto a larger "mother" vessel. Thousands of these barges or "lighters" are being distributed around the world. These will sail practically every navigable waterway to pick up and deliver cargo. The system is known as LASH, for Lighter Aboard SHip.

Commercial Submarines

While man has used the water for transportation purposes for thousands of years, during virtually all that time he has been effectively glued to its surface. Half a century ago, he began flying over its waves. Even here, in the air, lightning,

140

ice, hail, fog, and wind can be dangerous foes. Now, more and more, mariners are considering the approach taken by Jules Verne's fictional Captain Nemo, who, in his palacial submarine *Nautilus,* traveled at up to 50 mph in perfect comfort no matter how violent the environment above him. And Verne's *20,000 Leagues Under the Sea* was written way back in 1870!

The development of nuclear-powered ships, such as the American and West German merchant vessels *Savannah* and *Otto Hahn,* and the Russian icebreaker *Lenin,* as well as the experience gained in our nuclear submarines and in rapidly widening undersea exploration, may all point the way to use of the submarine for commercial shipping and travel. A giant, 300,000-ton submarine oil tanker has already been proposed. If this still seems unlikely to you, consider the following factors.

Commercial submarines traveling Arctic sea routes would greatly reduce the trading and traveling distances of the world. The present route from Tokyo to London is 12,800 miles; by polar passage (under the ice), it shrinks to 7,500 miles. Similarly, a ship traveling from Seattle to Oslo, Norway, via the Panama Canal, covers 10,700 miles; via the Arctic shortcut, the trip would only be 7,000 miles.

Then, of course, there is the advantage of not having to cope with the vagaries of the weather. If any of you have been through or even in the vicinity of a hurricane, you will appreciate being able to stay out of its way. I can recall being on the *Queen Mary,* one of the largest ships ever afloat, in the general area of a hurricane. Even that giant vessel was rolling and pitching to a considerable degree.

I can clearly remember watching my bathrobe, hanging on a hook behind the door of my stateroom, appear to swing out from the wall by 20 degrees or so, as the ship rolled away from it. Ropes had to be strung across all the decks to ensure safe passage across them, for in addition to sharp pitching and rolling, we had to contend with 60–80 mph winds. I can also remember the almost-empty dining room; most of the passengers had lost all desire to eat.

But the clearest image I have is that of an obviously seasoned traveler who was comfortably seated on a deck chair, wrapped in a blanket, and smoking a pipe. I admired his calm demeanor. Now, keep in mind the fact that this was taking place on the top deck, some 85 feet above the waterline. Suddenly, even as I watched, a giant wave broke over the deck, completely drenching the man, Fortunately, the wave had no strength at this height and he was not washed overboard. He sat there for a moment, tapped out his pipe, shrugged his shoulders, and went below.

An 85-foot wave! Clearly, even a surface-effect ship which travels ten feet above the water will have trouble managing a sea like that. The cruise ship *Queen of Bermuda* took a considerable beating during the same storm. One crewman was killed and a number of passengers were injured.

Another advantage of the submarine is that it doesn't *make* waves. This alone may make it possible for undersea craft to get up to very high speeds. Nuclear submarines already can maintain steady speeds of more than 30 mph (their actual speed is considered classified information by the government). Indeed, one of the Navy's main reasons for interest in hydrofoils and ACVs is that conventional surface craft have trouble keeping up with the fast subs.

Various kinds of research point toward underwater speeds of 100 mph and up. For example, it has long been known that the dolphin is able to move through water at top speed, hour after hour, with minimum effort. Even though subs don't make waves, they still create turbulence as they move through the water. The dolphins seem to have a complex body system which overcomes this and which permits what is called *laminar flow* along their bodies.

Part of the explanation lies in the animal's streamlined body contours. But his loose, rubber-like outer skin also has been found to play an important part in the process. There is even evidence that the dolphin employs a complex, brain-controlled system that provides laminar flow under various conditions by compensating for variations in pressure, density, temperature, and saltiness of the water, and even for current and the slow waves that sometimes occur below the surface.

In another attack on the problem of underwater speed, North American Aviation engineers are experimenting with various shapes which may be used in later craft. Speeds of 115 mph have already been achieved. One engineer has speculated on attaining speeds up to that of sound in water, or about 3,400 mph! David E. McNay, project engineer at North American, says this is something like attaining orbital speed in the atmosphere.

While this seems an unlikely possibility, new developments in light and high-strength materials may make super-stream-lining easier. (The strongest shape is inherently a sphere, which is clearly not a good shape for high-speed travel.) New developments in power generation, such as a thermo-nuclear fusion engine (a major step beyond even the current nuclear fission reactors), could supply the necessary power.*

Still other technical difficulties exist which must be overcome. Since light does not travel far in water, travel at high speeds will require other means of "seeing." New developments in the exciting field of three-dimensional laser photography, or holography, may point the way. Sonar (SOund Navigation And Ranging), which is now used, can tell us

---

* See *Energy in the World of the Future,* another book in this series, for details on fusion.

that something is in front of us, but not what it is. Engineers are investigating the potential of acoustical holography. Sound, after all, is a wave motion, just as light is; it may be possible to "see by sound," which travels better through the water than light does.

Navigation is another obstacle that is being surmounted with the aid of modern technology. Already in operation are devices which can navigate both air and sea craft with no reference whatever to the outside world. The method is called *inertial navigation* and is used on most of our large rockets and military aircraft, on all our nuclear subs, and on some of our larger commercial aircraft as well. The submarine *Nautilus*, which passed under the ice of the North Pole in 1958, was guided largely in this way.

Athelstan Spilhaus, scientist and author, points out:

> Although submarines have thus far been used principally for military purposes, the advantages of traveling below the disturbed interface between ocean and atmosphere with its waves, windstorms, and ice mean that submarine freight and passenger travel, as well as a variety of submarine vessels for research puposes, will undoubtedly be developed.

Any of these developments can help to make this prediction a reality, as can another one which some researchers have been considering for several years: a sub that can fly! A study was actually carried out by General Dynamics/Convair for the Bureau of Naval Weapons. Emphasis was placed on a moderate flying range of 300 to 500 miles, along with an underwater range of 50 miles at 6 mph and 75-foot depth capability. Engineers said the craft, which the Navy called the *Subplane*, would weigh 8 tons and would have a 500- to 1,500-pound payload. It would fly at 175 to 250 mph and would have a retractable ski to assist in takeoff.

While a missile has been developed that can do everything mentioned above and more, much work remains to be done before we see a *manned* flying sub. In the meantime, we might note that Japanese government and industry people have already collaborated on the design of a nuclear merchant submarine; it is now being studied for commercial feasibility. Large air-cushion and hydrofoil ships powered by nuclear reactors have also been proposed and have high potential for development.

On the other hand, some engineers believe that present-day nuclear power has not proved useful for today's commercial sea-going needs, that fusion is probably thirty or more years from practicality, and that we are in the midst of a developing fuel crisis. A German group suggests *wind-driven* merchant ships! These Dyna-Ships would not be the old-fashioned sailing ships, but would be computer-controlled and up-to-date in every respect. The sails would be set, reefed, and furled by machine and controlled by computer to take maximum advantage of wind and sea conditions. There would be auxiliary engines on board for windless times and to create electricity for onboard use.

The German engineers, and one or two groups here as well, believe that such ships would prove as reliable as fuel-driven ships, but would use far less fuel and would be more economical to run.

Could be.

9

Aircraft—
Up and Away

IN THE YEAR 1892 William Harben published a science-fiction story called "In the Year Ten Thousand."* He described our descendants, a race of beings which had evolved far beyond us—in intellect, in beauty, and in gentleness. He also had something to say about air travel. Remember that what you read now was written in 1892, eleven years before the Wright Brothers' flight:

> The old man and his son left the museum [where they were looking over such old-fashioned things as books, magazines, and pictures of our ugly faces] and walked into a wonderful park. Flowers of the most beautiful kinds and of sweetest fragrance grew on all sides. They came to a tall tower, four thousand feet in height, built of manufactured crystal. Something, like a great white bird, a thousand feet

* Reprinted in *Future Perfect, American Science Fiction of the Nineteenth Century,* by H. Bruce Franklin, Oxford University Press, N.Y., 1966.

long, flew across the sky and settled down on the tower's summit.

"This was one of the most wonderful inventions of the Seventieth Century," said the old man. "The early inhabitants of the earth could not have dreamed that it would be possible to go around it in twenty-four hours. In fact, there was a time when they were not able to go around it at all. Scientists were astonished when a man called Malburn, a great inventor, announced that, at a height of four thousand feet, he could disconnect an air ship from the laws of gravitation, and cause it to stand still in space till the earth had turned over."

In 1892 the farthest stretch of Harben's imagination saw 1,000 mph as the ultimate in speed. Yet today, more than eight thousand years before the 100th century, rockets attain speeds of 25,000 mph on flights to the moon and other planets; the manned rocket plane X-15 has exceeded 4,000 mph on short flights through the atmosphere; and operational military aircraft regularly fly at 2,000 mph. If it is really necessary, a man can easily get from New York to San Francisco in an hour and a half.

As we know, however, it still takes longer than that for the rest of us to get from New York to Boston or from San Francisco to Los Angeles. We have discussed one possible answer: high-speed ground transportation. But there are limitations to this approach; the high cost of guideway equipment and right-of-way limit its use to densely populated areas. Even a transcontinental tube-train would only have stops or branch-offs at the larger cities.

If we are to prevent our country from turning into a few gargantuan metropolitan areas, we must make the medium and small cities more accessible to one another and to the larger cities as well. Aircraft are marvelously flexible in that they need ground equipment, i.e., airports, only at the ends of the flight. However, with the rapid increases that have been taking place in flying, airports have been getting more and more crowded.

Yet a significant percentage of these travelers are making relatively short trips, which could perhaps be handled by other modes of transportation. Depending on the area, from 50 to 85 per cent of all air passengers are traveling less than 500 miles per trip. In the U.S., 30 per cent of the air passengers travel less than 300 miles. As far as the airlines are concerned, however, each trip still requires the same amount of space and handling at the two ends of the trip.

With more and more people traveling, and larger aircraft, airports are becoming larger and larger. Kennedy International Airport, serving the New York Metropolitan Area, is already crowded; yet it covers 7 1/2 square miles, an area equal to all of Manhattan Island south of 42nd Street. You don't put an airport like that in, or even very close to, a large city. (Kennedy Airport is 15 highway miles from the city, Newark Airport is 13, and LaGuardia 7). A fourth jetport is needed in the New York area, but large tracts of available land are becoming increasingly scarce. One favored area is 70 miles away from Manhattan.

Helicopters and V/STOLs

While helicopters are ideal for getting into and out of small areas vertically, they are slow in horizontal flight. Conventional aircraft are fine for covering horizontal distances swiftly, but they need large landing areas. What aviation has been seeking right along, and is still seeking, is aircraft that combine the most desirable features of the two.

Although the helicopter has been around for decades now, there are still major problems with it. It is noisy and it is slow, at least by comparison with conventional craft, which means less passenger-mile capability.

It is also expensive, both to buy and maintain. The main reason for this is the large rotor, which causes vibration problems. Sikorsky Aircraft is working on a system which is expected to isolate these vibrations, so that they will not be transmitted to the craft itself. This would also make for a quieter and smoother ride.

Nevertheless the helicopter has come a long way. Normal cruising speed in some of the larger passenger types can be as high as 140 mph, though normally it ranges around 100 mph or even less. For certain jobs, as where hovering for relatively long periods is required, it is unsurpassed. For such operations as rescue, construction, fire-fighting, and surveillance (wartime or traffic), it has proved itself many times over. One helicopter, the Sikorsky Skycrane, can haul a 20,000-pound load.

Helicopters are also useful for, and are used for, short passenger trips. New York Airways flies between the Wall Street Heliport in lower Manhattan and the major airports in the surrounding areas. Recently service was widened to include a smaller airport in Morristown, New Jersey.

While New York Airways is no longer subsidized by either the government or the airlines, its fare structure does include a sliding scale which depends on how much of the fare the connecting airline is willing to pick up. Thus the fare from the Wall Street Heliport to Kennedy International Airport ranges from $18 down to $12, and in the case of an international flight, it might be free! The airlines consider the helicopter flights a service that helps theirs, and are willing to pay for it. The trip takes 12 to 14 minutes, as opposed to one hour for the bus ride from Manhattan. (On the other hand, the bus ride costs $2.50.)

In 1972 New York Airways carried 400,000 passengers,

30-passenger Sikorsky operating in New York City.

150

up from 190,000 in 1966. Although this was only a tiny fraction of the city's more than 37 million air travelers, the company turned a profit for the first time—perhaps the only time a regularly scheduled helicopter passenger service has been able to do this.

The company is counting on increasing acceptance of the service, and increasing congestion on the ground, to provide even greater patronage in the coming years.

Naturally, prices could come down if more people used the service. On the other hand, one can never be sure that more widely available service would result in the kind of patronage that would be required to support it. But planners are inclined to feel that this would occur.

A project that was proposed a few years ago could help: a monumental structure which would serve as a transportation terminal, with heliport facilities. The idea is similar in principle to the Cornell Aeronautical Laboratory concept, the Master Mode-mixer, shown on the next two pages.

To be located on the East River, which runs along the east side of Manhattan, the eight-storied building would cover two large city blocks and a bit of the river. Tentative plans provide parking space for up to 2,000 cars, facilities for baggage and cargo-handling airline offices, taxi and bus ramps, and connections on the river for hydrofoil craft. Since part of the building would extend out over the river, most of the helicopter departures and approaches could be made over water, which would certainly minimize a current problem of noise in the CBD.

The large, flat roof would be able to handle a number of the 70-plus passenger 'copters now being planned. These will be much more economical to run than today's smaller models. The cost of flying 70 passengers in one craft is obviously far less than for 20 passengers in two different craft. With improvements in instrument flying, which would provide re-

The Master Mode-Mixer: An all-transport terminal.

liable flights even in poor weather, the new service should attract new passengers.

If other cities should follow suit, there is the even more attractive prospect of direct flights, at 180 mph or faster, between city centers several hundred miles apart throughout the country.

For the super-cities of the future, this may be a way of reducing airport, as well as road, congestion. Cities such as Washington, Baltimore, Boston, and Philadelphia account for almost 30 per cent of all domestic passenger traffic in the New York airports. If CBD-to-CBD vertical take-off and landing (VTOL) service is instituted in these cities, a substantial share of the load on the airports and on the airport roads could be eliminated.

Sikorsky Aircraft has proposed an intriguing plan which is reminiscent of the road/rail systems we discussed in Chapter Seven. In the Skybus program, a large Sikorsky Flying Crane would carry a detachable passenger pod. At either end of the flight, the pod could operate as a bus—either self-propelled or drawn by a tractor—with all the advantages that normal bus travel offers. In effect, we have a VTOL bus.

Another term you may have seen is STOL, which stands for *short* takeoff and landing. STOLs look like conventional aircraft, but depend on powerful engines and special lifting and stabilization devices for landing and takeoff. These might include large retractable flaps to increase wing area at low speeds and to deflect the airstream downward for increased lift.

Being faster than helicopters but requiring more space to land, STOLs might be used in intercity operations between suburban airports. It should be noted, however, that all the VTOL carft we shall describe shortly can also operate in the STOL mode where landing space is available. Thus, you might see some of them designated V/STOL.

All VTOLs pose difficult technical problems. While an ordinary aircraft can develop lift slowly by increasing speed along a runway, the VTOL must take off without this kind of help. It seeks all its initial lift without any forward speed. This requires a great amount of lifting power, which is likely to be needed only for takeoff and landing. The result is lower payload, higher costs, and shorter range. Typical range for a helicopter is only a few hundred miles.

Operating costs are improving, but are still higher than those of conventional aircraft. Nevertheless, for reasons given earlier, there is no question that there is a place for VTOLs. Many feel that the medium-range market, in the 100–500 mile region operating from city center to city center, is where the VTOL will make its greatest mark—assuming a satisfactory design can be found.

One reason for the slowness of the typical chopper is the fact that the large rotor is used for both horizontal and vertical flight. In some models, the craft simply "leans" forward for horizontal flight, thus transferring some of the thrust from the vertical to the horizontal direction. In others, the more complicated approach of varying the pitch of the blades as they sweep around is used. Although pure helicopters have gotten up to well over 200 mph, very high power is required. These craft, therefore, are very inefficient at high speed.

Unlike standard aircraft, larger engines and streamlining are not the answer. The critical factor is the rotor. In addition to aerodynamic problems in high-speed rotation, the rotor is large and can only take so much speed of rotation before it tears itself to pieces.

The development and substitution of turbine engines for conventional piston engines has been useful, however. (We mentioned this type of engine earlier, in connection with the New York-Boston TurboTrain). The weight of a helicopter turbine engine is less than half that of a piston engine producing the same horsepower. Hence, the craft can carry a greater payload; it can also carry two engines, either of which provides enough power to support it. Thus, there is a built-in safety factor.

Since the rotor can't be speeded up past a certain point, other approaches to higher speeds are necessary. For example, the power of the rotor can be augmented by the addition of a separate means of driving the craft in forward motion. The result is a hybrid, or compound, helicopter. The rotor of a compound craft is powered as usual for takeoff; when the desired altitude is reached, power is transferred to a conventional propeller or jet for forward thrust. At this point, the rotor is allowed to freewheel, that is, spin freely, as the craft moves through the air. This provides some lift, but not enough. Stubby wings are used for additional lift.

While the compound is an advance (speeds of well over 275 mph have been reached), it is not an ideal solution. The freewheeling rotor is more hindrance than aid; and the wings, stubby though they may be, interfere with the downwash action of the main rotor in vertical flight. The additional weight of the wings and drive units also detracts from payload.

A number of different kinds of VTOL have been built (see photos) or are under study. An obvious possibility is to tilt the rotor or rotors forward, once the desired altitude has been achieved in vertical flight. While this is not practicable with the usual single large rotor, or even the tandem design (one behind the other), a pair of rotors at the wing tips has been tried with good success.

Another possibility is to stop the rotor, fold it, and perhaps stow it away during cruise flight. Such a design promises greatly improved speed. However, the system would be complicated and probably heavy. Also, wind-tunnel tests have

World's largest non-helicopter VTOL: the X-142A.

Bell Aerosystems' X-22A.

shown that the rotor is tricky to stop and start in forward flight. When the blade slows down below freewheeling speed, it loses the rigidity imparted by its spin and starts flopping around, sometimes quite violently.

A possible way out is to redesign the rotor and to make it part of the aircraft's fixed wing structure during forward flight. Hughes Tool Company engineers maintain that a potential speed of 500 mph is possible with such a configuration.

For the stowed-rotor design, assuming good streamlining can be achieved, there appears to be no practical limit on speed. Some feel, however, that sufficient rotor strength with practical weight for the conversion process can't be achieved with today's materials. Super-strength materials, now in development, could be the answer here.

One example, which consists of tiny, thread-like boron filiments embedded in an epoxy plastic base, provides light weight, high stiffness, and good corrosion resistance. Used until now only as a test material on the F-111 jet fighter, it has been approved for its first commercial application: replacement of an existing part on the leading wing edge of an aircraft.

Boron fibers are more than twice as stiff as steel, yet are less than a third as dense. When they are put into a plastic or metal matrix (surrounding material), they form a composite with a stiffness per unit weight that is much higher than that of steel. The fibers are also very strong. A 190-mile length of boron fiber could support itself without breaking; the strength of steel is thus also exceeded on a weight-for-weight basis. Clearly, such a strong material will be very useful in high speed helicopter rotors, whether stowed or not.

Ling-Temco-Vought, whose entry into the experimental VTOL field is probably the furthest along, has provided us with the X-142A—the largest VTOL in the world (page 157). The commercial version, when and if built, would be called the Downtowner. In this design, four smaller rotors are used, and wings as well as rotors tilt. While it appears cumbersome, the aerodynamic features of this design appear to be very satisfactory. The present aircraft already has the capability of carrying 44 passengers at cruising speeds of more than 300 mph.

In a rather different approach from the Downtowner, the Bell Aerosystems X-22A (also shown on page 157) uses smaller rotors enclosed in ducts. Company engineers maintain that the ducted units increase the thrust of the props during takeoff and landing, and serve as lifting surfaces during forward flight. With one eye on safety, they have designed the craft to be able to maintain vertical flight with one engine out. As in the X-142A, the craft can cruise in horizontal flight with any two engines turning all four props, through a system of gears and clutches (all of which add weight and complexity).

Top speed of this craft is about 325 mph, but the Bell people believe that a speed of 450 mph and even higher is a possibility. (Maximum speed of the X-142A is 430 mph.) We have already mentioned Hughes' prediction of 500 mph for its stopped-rotor design. But why stop here?

Another type of VTOL is called the fan-in-wing. The XV-5A, for example, has a five-foot diameter fan embedded in each stubby wing. For vertical lift, valves close the jet engine tail pipes used in horizontal flight. The gases are diverted to the fan blades in the wing, causing them to spin and generate lift. This increases the thrust of the gases at the expense of speed, which, of course, is not needed for landing or takeoff anyway. Thus, relatively small quantities of high-speed gases are converted by the fans into large quantities of lower energy, high-mass air flow. Maximum speed has already been demonstrated to be 547 mph, and range is about 1,000 miles.

All the craft we have discussed so far have had vertical lift capability "tacked" on to conventional airframes (or vice versa, if you prefer). The future may see even more novel designs.

A model of the strange-looking ADAM II has already been built and is being tested (page 161). ADAM stands for Air Deflection And Modulation. Turbofan engines will be located right in the wings and nose, as shown. To obtain upward thrust, the fixed-wing design diverts air flow downward through a series of louvers or slats. ADAM is planned as a high-subsonic craft, which may bring it into the 600-mph class.

Finally, as if you didn't expect it, work is proceeding on several supersonic, jet-driven VTOLs. These, as well as the XV-5A and ADAM, are the kind of high-performance aircraft that must sacrifice payload and economy of operation to obtain this high performance. Therefore, for the time being at least, they are of more interest to the military than to commercial operators.

Jumbo Jets

As has happened so often in the past, however, what the military does today is put into commercial use tomorrow. A good example is that of the jumbo, or giant, jets. Originally conceived as a giant military transport or cargo plane (the Lockheed C-5A), these football-field-size craft begin to rival the thousand-foot airship mentioned by William Farben, and have already begun to revolutionize the air transportation business. They double, triple, or even quadruple the capacity of the largest of yesterday's jets, which were already pretty big.

So gigantic is the C-5A that shaving one-thousandth of an inch off the thickness of the paint would save 2,000 pounds

Tomorrow's ADAM II.

The Lockheed L-1011 TriStar, newest jumbo jet.

of weight. It has a length of 246 feet, a wingspread of 222 feet, and the tail is 65 feet high—roughly six stories tall.

The first of the jumbo jets to go into commercial service was the Boeing 747. It has a capacity of 350 to more than 400 passengers (depending on fuel load and seating arrangements), and is slightly faster than the standard jet liner. The big change, however, is in passenger comfort, made possible by the generous proportions of the plane. The cabin, 190 feet long by 20 feet wide, is about twice as long and half again as wide as the cabin of the Boeing 707. While there are many more seats, they are wider and more generously spaced, or are supposed to be, anyway. There have been complaints to the contrary. The 747s, which went into service in 1970, now cost $25 million apiece.

There were of course problems at first. Running 350 passengers through customs operations designed for much smaller craft, as well as handling the vast amount of baggage involved, produced some giant-sized headaches. But these are being solved as new facilities are built and others modified.

A big advantage of these craft is that there are fewer of them taking off and landing, and fewer in the air at any one time for ground controllers to worry about. In addition, larger craft should provide economies in operation, all of which should help hold the line on otherwise spiraling costs.

The jumbo jets will undoubtedly accelerate the swing from ocean to air travel that has been taking place all along. In a survey taken a few years ago, it was found that 86 per cent of all people who traveled overseas flew, as compared to 68 per cent ten years earlier.

Within the last decade one of the largest steamship companies, Cunard, has retired the two largest liners in the world, the *Queen Mary* and the *Queen Elizabeth,* plus several smaller ones, because of rising costs and falling patronage.

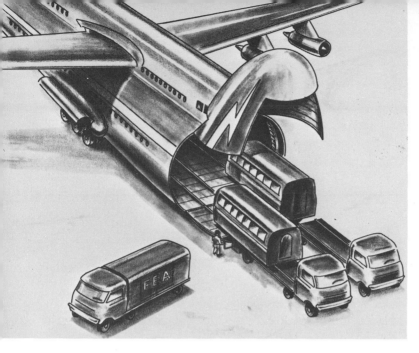

Ford's futuristic Air Bus.

No one expects ocean travel to disappear entirely, however. For those who have the time, the delights of an ocean voyage are undeniable. Perhaps surface effect ships on a large scale could turn the tide. In the meantime, Cunard has built a conventional luxury liner, the *Queen Elizabeth II*, which is smaller and more efficient than the old one.

The Federal Aviation Administration forecasts a total United States airline fleet of 3,600 planes by 1984, an increase of 1,000 over 1973. Of these they expect jumbo liners to make up 60 per cent of these craft and to account for 80 per cent of the seats.

The great size and payload capacity of these giant planes will probably lead to some unusual applications, as, for example, the Ford Motor Company's idea for an Air Bus. Computer-dispatched buses would pick up air passengers near their homes or offices and would transfer them directly into

163

aircraft at the airports. The process would be reversed at the landing points. This would cut down on ground congestion and parking problems; it would also eliminate the long walks to and from parking lots and other delays typically encountered in the ground/air transfer process.

It is on giant craft like these, too, that the first application of *nuclear propulsion* for aircraft will be seen. At ranges above 5,000 miles, a large nuclear-powered aircraft can carry a larger payload than a chemically powered airplane of the same takeoff weight.

However, many technical problems remain to be solved before we see the advent of such craft. Among them is the need to include energy-absorbing structures that would enable the nuclear reactors to withstand possible crash impacts without releasing deadly radiation.

We probably won't see such craft for ten or more years. What we have already seen, however, is another kind of super-jet, the supersonic transport, or SST.

Faster Than Sound

A supersonic aircraft is defined as one that travels faster than the speed of sound. This speed varies with altitude, but is about 670 mph. Supersonic military craft have been around for years. And five years ago, when the first edition of this book was published, it looked like we were entering the supersonic era with a bang (forgive the pun). A British-French team has indeed come up with the Concorde, and the Russians with their TU-144. Both are Mach 2 aircraft, meaning that they travel at twice the speed of sound, or about 1,350 mph.

The American air industry, with considerable funding from the government, had decided to leap ahead with an even larger, faster (Mach 3) aircraft. With three times the speed and twice the capacity of the Boeing 707, the SST was expected to do for the Pacific what the subsonic jets did for the Atlantic—namely, shrink the time between countries and tie the Far East more closely into world affairs.

In the Western hemisphere, this craft would bring South America as close to the United States, and Africa as close to Europe, as the earlier jets brought Europe and America. New York to Buenos Aires becomes a five-hour trip—less than it takes to Paris today—rather than a bone-wearing eleven.

But the rising tide of environmental considerations changed the boom of the SST to a whimper. Actually there were a number of reasons, but the major factors were environmental. One problem had to do with increasing fears that water vapor or nitrogen oxides from the SST exhaust might cause deterioration of the earth's ozone layer, thereby exposing life on earth to high, dangerous levels of ultraviolet radiation.

Then there is the fact that a craft which travels faster through the atmosphere than the speed of sound generates a shock wave that drags along behind it and produces what is known as the sonic boom. While in no way dangerous to a person in good health, the loud crack could be harmful to nervous and ill people, and be simply unacceptable to others. As a result, the F.A.A. has outlawed supersonic flight over the United States by civilian aircraft. Thus (once SSTs begin to operate in this country) we shall see once again the ironic situation of New York being "closer" to London than it is to Los Angeles (three hours vs. five in a Mach 3 craft) just as it was before the transcontinental railroad was built.

This restriction has another disadvantage, particularly for a fixed-wing craft like the French-British Concorde. Because the Concorde's wings are designed for supersonic flight, they are not efficient in subsonic flight. This will mean high

The British-French supersonic Concorde 002 in flight over Southern England.

fuel costs for overland flights. The Boeing SST was designed to get around this by use of a "swing-wing" concept. With wings fully spread, control and handling would be better than even today's subsonic jets, with their partially swept-back wings. For high-speed flight, the wings would be swung fully back, providing good aerodynamic characteristics for 1,800-mph cruising at high altitudes. Thus the plane would have obtained the best of two quite different worlds—but at the cost of added weight and complexity.

A flight from Chicago to Paris might operate like this: From Chicago to the east coast, the SST would operate subsonically, with wings in the intermediate position. As the craft headed out over the Atlantic, the wings would glide smoothly back into the sleek delta position and the craft would accelerate to almost three times the speed of sound (1,800 mph). Near the end of the trip, as the coast of Europe was approached, the process would be reversed.

Another type of swing-wing has been proposed, but it is unbelievably radical. As shown in the illustration, instead of both wings gliding back into a delta position, the entire wing would rotate about 45 degrees as a unit, so that in the high-speed position the wing on one side would be pointing in the direction of flight while the other pointed toward the rear! All our ideas of symmetry go out the window. The developer, Dr. R. T. Jones of the NASA Ames Research Center, feels that this may be the way to achieve commercial supersonic capability without the penalties of high fuel

A radical design for supersonic flight. The wing outline in this artist's concept shows how the wing would be positioned for take-off (straight) and high-speed flight.

consumption other SSTs must pay. Tests indicate that such an aircraft would require only about one-fourth the takeoff energy now needed by comparable delta-wing jet transports with similar payloads. This of course would also cut down on noise, which is a major problem with SSTs. In all likelihood this design would be held, at least at first, to Mach 1.5; and the craft is expected to be able to cruise overland at Mach 1.2 without producing a sonic boom.

In a different kind of approach to the noise problem, we might see a plane that takes off powered by relatively quiet fan-jets, and then switches over to pure-jet in high-altitude cruise flight.

Administration officials in the United States government are convinced that the United States must have an SST of its own, and even though the Boeing SST was canceled, SST work has not died out completely by any means. Basic research on supersonic flight, and its effects on the environment, continues, though at a much reduced level. If the various problems can be licked, we are likely to see a revival of the program on a large scale.

HST

The belief held by aeronautical engineers and airline planners—namely, that whenever speed is offered people will take it—has led to plans for craft even faster than the SST. The next step is the HST, the hypersonic transport. And a dazzling concept it is, for we are now talking of speeds of 4,000 and 5,000 mph through the upper atmosphere!

The fastest flights so far have been made by the X-15, mentioned at the beginning of this chapter. On November 18, 1966, the X-15-2 hit 4,250 mph, a new record for manned atmospheric flight. But the X-15 is a rocket craft and carries

The Hypersonic Transport, or HST.

fuel for only a few short minutes of powered flight. For short experimental flights, this is fine; for longer trips and higher payloads within the atmosphere, other forms of propulsion, such as the ramjet, are necessary.

The ramjet lies somewhere between the jet and the rocket. The next step, supersonic combustion ramjets, or *scramjets*, may even play a role in sending payloads into space.

If, as discussed earlier, fossil fuels must be phased out, hydrogen may become the fuel of the future. The light weight of hydrogen in combination with its high energy value

169

gives it the highest energy density per pound of all fuels. A hypersonic, hydrogen-fueled aircraft has already been proposed. Not only would the super-cold liquid hydrogen be a good fuel, it would also provide an answer to the continuing problem in high-speed flight—frictional heating due to air resistance. Temperatures of leading edges can go up into the thousands of degrees, possibly causing weakening of structural members. The liquid hydrogen, at −423° F, could be used to help cool these areas.

Someday in the future, even the X-15 may seem like the prop-driven plane seems to us now—slow and a bit old-fashioned. Plans are already on the drawing board for aircraft capable of a speed of 11,000 mph.

And why not? Materials technology is advancing rapidly and may well provide substances able to stand up against the multi-thousand degree temperatures that will be encountered. Programs are already under way to develop a hypersonic test engine and to develop and test lightweight structures capable of operating at high speeds.

While all of this sounds rather far away at the moment, there is no theoretical reason why these or even higher speeds cannot be attained. Some aircraft experts predict we will see such craft in service by 1985 or 1990.

At 18,000 mph, however, the craft has reached orbital speed. And at 25,000 mph, the problem is no longer how to keep it up, but how to keep it *down*—that is, how to keep it from flying off into space.

Even at 11,000 mph—which can probably be attained without any revolutionary development, such as a tunnel through the earth—no two cities on earth would be more than three-quarters of an hour apart. How small would our world be then?

Epilogue

LAST TRUCK GRINDS TO HALT IN NORTHEAST CORRIDOR
ALL ROADS CLOGGED   SOME SUPPLIES ALREADY SHORT
EFFORTS TO CLEAR ROADS AND HIGHWAYS FAIL
MILLIONS OF CARS AND TRUCKS STRANDED
PRESIDENT DECLARES NATIONAL EMERGENCY,
TO SPEAK TONIGHT

THIS MIGHT BE the headline in your newspaper ten or twenty years from now. Don't think for a moment that it can't happen. On December 30, 1963, traffic in the heart of Boston did grind to a halt—and it stayed that way for more than five hours. Other severe tie-ups occurred in 1967 and 1969. With ever-larger agglomerations of people and cars a virtual certainty, at least in the near future, such tie-ups are likely to *increase* rather than diminish, and to increase in intensity—unless something is done about the situation now.

It is important to realize that one of the major objectives of looking into the future is to foresee the bad as well as the good. The point is that *both* are possible. For there is not *a* future—settled, solid, inexorable. There are many futures.

Perhaps this needs clarification. Look at it this way: The future is not "there," waiting for time to uncover it. The future is as formless and colorless as a lump of clay. It is what we, all of us, will make of it. I wrote an optimistic book, but not because I think that is the way life will be in the future. I wrote it that way because that is the way we must make it be.

By showing what the future could be like, as in the Prologue, by showing that man need not be ignored or left out
even in a "supermachine" age, I have tried to show what and
how much still remains to be done. The fantastic promise of
machines and computers can be, and must be, put to use for
the comfort, aid, and use of the human. This is what new
developments should be all about.

If we destroy our cities in an attempt to improve transportation, we shall be moving faster and faster, but from nowhere to nowhere. Indeed, behind every discussion of technology must stand the idea that the system must serve the
people. Or, as Robert H. Cannon, Jr., Assistant Secretary of
Transportation, put it, "A really good transportation system can serve as an instrument for improving the structure
of society itself."

In this book, we have considered a number of possible
solutions to a difficult, complex, and nagging set of problems. Some of the solutions are complex, others are expensive, most are impractical—now. But I dare anyone to point
to a single approach and say, "It can't be done."

For example, a giant cargo container can travel directly
from a warehouse in Chicago to another in the heart of France
without any layovers and without ever having to be unpacked.
Once placed on the truck trailer, it can travel directly to
dockside and be swung, as shown, right onto a ship (or plane).
At the other end, it can be transferred to a train as well as
a truck. The savings in time, effort, and expense are obvious.

This technique is known as *containerized shipping* and
has been called "the greatest advance in freight movement
since Railway Express." The point, of course, is that if this
kind of "systemized" transportation can be accomplished for
the transportation of goods, surely a way can be found to do
it for humans.

One possible approach, the *traveling cartridge,* has been

Containerized Shipping.

proposed by the brilliant and wide-ranging architect engineer, R. Buckminster Fuller. As you can see, the privacy
and flexibility of the automobile is combined with the mani-
fold possibilities and advantages of public transport. Clearly,
however, there would be a considerable weight penalty in the
extra motors, wheels, and car bodies that would have to be
carried in the public transport modes. New developments in
lightweight, super-strength materials might overcome this
objection. A more persistent problem would be the difficulty
in meshing the various aspects of such a many-sided system.

Perhaps aerospace management techniques for attacking
large-scale problems and integrating large-scale operations

can be applied here on earth, as well as in building, launching, and tracking 6-million-pound rockets. Indeed, it may yet turn out that one of the greatest contributions of the aerospace industry will be the management and planning techniques that will make a reliable, flexible, and balanced transportation system a reality.

Concurrent with the development of these techniques has been the growth of computers which permit the storing, handling, and consideration of vast quantities of data. Myron Miller, of the Department of Transportation, says that the

R. Buckminster Fuller's Traveling Cartridge.

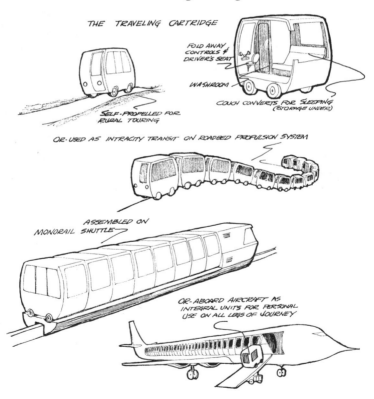

old ways of piecemeal planning are obsolete. More important, he points out, is the fact that with developments in computer engineering, new mathematical techniques, and the ability to make better trade-off and cost studies, we can for the first time begin to look at the larger problems.

Regional planning, for instance, has become an accepted method of attacking these problems. Such organizations as the Metropolitan Transportation Authority (MTA)—covering New Jersey, New York, and Connecticut—make sense in that all modes of travel for a large region can be pulled together.

Among the plans of the MTA are major improvements and extensions of subways and commuter trains, additional airports plus better access to new and existing ones, as well as giant transportation terminals in the heart of the city, and in outlying districts. Included also are plans for new midtown and downtown distribution system employing one or more of the techniques we have mentioned, such as moving sidewalks, rail cars, people movers, and so on.

It is an exciting prospect. For the first time, there is at least hope that the large-scale problem can be faced squarely and, perhaps, licked.

Bibliography

BOOKS

Buel, R. A., *Dead End: the Automobile in Mass Transportation*, Prentice-Hall, 1972.

Burby, John, *Great American Motion Sickness: Or Why You Can't Get There from Here*, Little, Brown, 1971.

Calder, N., ed., *The World in 1984*, Penguin Books, 1965 (vols. 1 & 2).

Caldwell, W. A., *How to Save Urban America*, New American Library, 1973 (paperback).

Danforth, P. M., *Transportation: Managing Man on the Move*, Doubleday, 1970.

Dept. of Audio-Visual Education, *Personal Rapid Transit*, University of Minnesota (proceedings of a conference held November 1–3, 1971).

Farris, M. T., and P. T. McElhiney, *Modern Transportation: Selected Readings*, 2nd ed. Houghton-Mifflin, 1973.

Gunston, W. T., *Hydrofoils and Hovercraft: New Vehicles for Sea and Land*, Doubleday, 1970.

———, *Transportation: Problems and Prospects*, Dutton, 1972.

Hellman, H., *Helicopters and Other VTOLs*, Doubleday, 1970.

Leavitt, Helen, *Superhighway-Superhoax*, Doubleday, 1970.

Massachusetts Institute of Technology, *Project Metran: Boston 1990*, MIT Press, 1967.

McLeod, Sterling, and Science Book Associates Editors, *How We Will Move All the People: Transportation for Tomorrow's World*, Messner, 1971.

Mowbray, A., *Road to Ruin*, Lippincott, 1969.

Reische, Diana, *Problems of Mass Transportation*, Wilson, 1970.

Richards, Brian, *New Movement in Cities*, Reinhold, 1966.

Ross, Frank, Jr., *Transportation of Tomorrow*, Lothrop Lee & Shepard, 1968.

Schneider, K. R., *Autokind vs. Mankind: an Analysis of Tyranny, a Proposal for Rebellion, a Plan for Reconstruction*, Norton, 1971.

Stone, T. R., *Beyond the Automobile: Reshaping the Transportation Environment*, Prentice-Hall, 1971.

Williams, E. W., Jr., ed., *Future of American Transportation*, Prentice-Hall, 1971.

BOOKLETS, REPORTS AND SYMPOSIUM PROCEEDINGS

Brower, W. B., Jr., *Tubeflight—A Review*, reprint from the Proceedings of the Seventh Space Congress, April 1970, Rensselaer Polytechnic Institute, June 1970.

Cautley, Paul, *Inter-City and the Advanced Passenger Train*, Society of Automotive Engineers #730059, reprint of a paper presented at a meeting held January 8–12, 1973.

Cornell Aeronautical Laboratory (now Calspan Corp.), *Metrotran-2000—A Study of Future Concepts in Metropolitan Transportation for the Year 2000*, October 1967 (Buffalo, N.Y.).

Hoel, L. A., *Technological and Institutional Innovations in European Urban Transport*, Carnegie-Mellon University, December 1972.

177

Hoffman, G. A., *On Minimizing the Land Used by Automobiles and Buses in the Urban Central Core: Underground Highways and Parking Facilities,* Rand Corporation Report #P-3002, October 1964 (Santa Monica, California).

Office of Administrative Operations, *Urban Mass Transportation, Bibliographic List No. 6,* U.S. Department of Transportation, September 1971.

Secretary of Transportation, *Sixth Annual Report on the High Speed Ground Transportation Act of 1965,* 1973.

————, *Fifth Report on the High Speed Ground Transportation Act of 1965,* 1971.

Transportation Technology, Inc., *An Introduction to Personal Rapid Transit Systems of Transportation Technology, Inc.,* Denver, Colo., February 1973.

Urban Mass Transportation Administration, *An Urban Transportation Bibliography,* U.S. Department of Transportation, May 3, 1971.

U.S. Department of Transportation, *America on the Move,* undated.

————, *Fifth Annual Report,* 1971.

————, *First Annual Report on the Implementation of the Statement on National Transportation Policy,* May 1972.

————, *A Statement on National Transportation Policy,* 1971.

————, *Urban Transportation Needs,* (eight lectures), 1972.

————, *U.S. Department of Transportation—Facts and Functions,* January 1, 1971 (U.S. Government Printing Office 5000–0049).

ARTICLES

American City, "Transpo '72: New Equipment Advances Promise Improved Transportation Systems," *American City,* November 1972.

Anderson, J. E., "PRT: Urban Transportation of the Future?" *The Futurist,* February 1973.

Asimov, Isaac, "Life in 1990," *Science Digest,* August 1965.

Avery, W. H., "Beyond the Supersonic Transport," *Science and Technology,* February 1968.

Aviation Week, "Magnetic Force Studied for Intercity Travel," *Aviation Week,* March 22, 1971.

Ayres, R. V., "Urban Transportation of the Future," *The Futurist,* August 1968.

Barloon, M. J., "The Coming of the Super-Railroad," *Harper's Magazine,* April 1967.

Barris, George, "Automobiles 40 Years From Today," *Science and Mechanics,* March 1970.

Bernstein, V. H., "Our Transportation System That Gets Us Nowhere," *Redbook,* March 1971.

Brown, D. A., "Advanced SST Concepts Studied," *Aviation Week and Space Technology,* January 17, 1972.

Burck, C. G., "Little Railroad That Could; Lindenwold Line," *Fortune,* July 1971.

Business Week, "Showcase for Integrated Transport: Newark-Elizabeth Complex," *Business Week,* November 27, 1971.

————, "SST's Point of No Return," *Business Week,* February 27, 1971.

————, "The Test Flights of the High Speed Trains," *Business Week,* February 24, 1973.

178

———, "Why America May Become a Parking Lot," *Business Week*, October 17, 1970.

Cherington, P. (interview), "Transportation Mess: Some Practical Solutions," *Forbes*, January 1, 1971.

Chilton, F., and others, "Magnetic Levitation: Tomorrow's Transportation," *Bulletin of the Atomic Scientists*, March 1972.

Creedy, J. A., "Nationalization of the Transportation System," *Vital Speeches of the Day*, March 15, 1972.

Driscoll, E., "Propulsion for the 1980's," *Science News*, January 9, 1971.

———, STOL Aircraft for the Late 1970's, *Science News*, April 17, 1971.

Dyckman, J. W., "Transportation in Cities," *Scientific American*, September 1965.

The Editors, "An Electric Solution to the Traffic Problem," *Esquire*, February 1969.

Edwards, L. K., "High Speed Tube Transportation," *Scientific American*, August 1965.

Evans, G. G., and K. V. Kordesch, "Hydrazine-Air Fuel Cells," *Science*, December 1, 1967.

Ewan, T. K., "Supersonic Combustion for Sustained Hypersonic Flight," *Naval Engineer's Journal*, August 1967.

Fenton, R. E., and K. W. Olson, "The Electronic Highway," *IEEE Spectrum*, July 1969.

Fortune, "Mass Transportation: Future Technologies," *Fortune*, April 1972.

———, "U.S. Transportation System and How to Make It Run" (symposium, with editorial comment), *Fortune*, July 1971.

Gas Turbine World, "MTA to Test Turbo-Electric Rail Cars in Revenue Service," *Gas Turbine World*, June 1972.

Gates, S. B., "The All-Wing Aircraft," *New Scientist*, May 27, 1965.

Gilmore, C. P., "How You'll Drive the Amazing Urbmobile," *Popular Science*, October 1967.

Gwynne, P., "Transportation of Joy," *New Scientist*, November 9, 1972.

Handling and Shipping, "Transportation Technology," *Handling and Shipping*, January 1971, 1972, 1973.

Hanson, R. J., "High Speed Ground Transportation," *Journal of the Boston Society of Engineers*, October 1966.

Hawkins, W. M., "The Next 50 Years in Aviation," *Astronautics & Aeronautics*, July 1965.

Hohenemser, K. H., "Aircraft in the Balance: STOL/VTOL concept," *Environment*, December 1971.

Holder, Fred, "The Computer-Controlled Auto," *Science and Mechanix*, March 1970.

Howard, T. E., "Rapid Excavation," *Scientific American*, November 1967.

Kallis, S. A., Jr., "Leapfrogging the SST: An Alternative," *National Review*, April 20, 1971.

Kocivar, Ben, "Jumbo Jetfoil Will Be Super-Fast, Super-Smooth," *Popular Science*, April 1973.

———, "QUESTOL: a New Kind of Jet for Short Hops," *Popular Science*, May 1972.

———, "Surface Effect Ships," *Popular Science*, July 1971.

———, "Why We Must Get Back on the Tracks," *Congressional Record*, November 8, 1972.

Mumford, L., "In Praise of Trains," *Harper's Magazine*, August 1972.

Newsweek, "Auto-Train Miracle," *Newsweek*, January 3, 1972.

Packer, R. E., "The Automated Processing of People," *Computers and Automation*, April 1966.

Peterson, W. C., "1972 Urban Vehicle Design Competition: They Plan to Win with Hydrogen," *Popular Mechanics*, August 1973.

Popular Mechanics, "How We'll Keep 'Em Moving," *Popular Mechanics*, April 1972.

Road Test, "The Unbeatable Combination" (re Wankel-powered Mazda), *Road Test, March* 1973.

Scott, D., "New No-Wheels Train Gets a Lift from Magnetic," *Popular Science*, January 1972.

Shaman, D., and H. Shaman, "Up, Up and Away! Very Slowly" (air-ships), *Popular Mechanics*, February 1972.

Spiegal, M., "Air Cushions Go to Work," *Mechanix Illustrated*, May 1972.

Time, "Showdown on the SST," *Time*, March 29, 1971.

U.S. News and World Report, "Can Northeast Avert a Transport Crisis?" *U.S. News and World Report*, September 27, 1971.

———, "Drive for Modern Navy, Warships That Fly: Surface Effect Ships," *U.S. News and World Report*, December 6, 1971.

———, "Riding on Air: U.S. Train of the Future," *U.S. News and World Report*, March 15, 1971.

von Braun, W., "NASA's New Mach 1 Airliner: Advanced Technology Transport," *Popular Science*, April 1972.

Ward, E. J., "Merger of Ground Transportation and Automobiles," *Rail International*, February 1970.

Wahl, P., "Transportation Muddle: There Must Be a Better Way to Get from Here to There," *Popular Science*, May 1972.

Whitelaw, A. H., "Future Polar Transport," *Sea Front*, July 1970.

Winchester, J. H., "Airplanes That Fly from Downtown," *Readers' Digest*, February 1971.

Wyman, B. W., "Transportation in the 1970s: Years of Crisis," *Handling and Shipping*, January 1970.

Yaffee, M. L., "Magnetic Vehicle R & D Spurred," *Aviation Week & Space Technology*, July 10, 1972.

———, "NASA Building STOL Transports," *Aviation Week*, September 13, 1971.

Index

Acceleration-deceleration. *See* specific systems

Accidents. *See* Safety and accidents

ADAM II, 160, 161

Advanced Concept Train (ACT), 35

Advanced Passenger Train (APT), 43-45

Aerial Transport System, 30-31

Air bags, 88

Air Bus, 163-64

Air-Cushion Vehicles (ACVs), 5-6, 47-54 (*See also* Project Tubeflight); Surface Effect Ship (SES), 134-40

Air Gulper. *See* Project Tubeflight

Air jets, 63ff.

Air pollution (fumes), 16, 90-97; in tubes or tunnels, 61, 89, 112-13

Aircraft (planes), 40, 146-70. (*See also* Airports; Helicopters); fatalities, 60; *Subplane,* 144

Airplanes. *See* Aircraft; Airports

Airports, 13, 28, 30-31, 39, 105, 148ff. (*See also* specific airports); Air Bus and, 164

Alden StaRRcar, 123, 124, 128

Alexandria, Va., 113

Alkali-metal batteries, 97

AMTRAK, 39

Anderson, J. Edward, 109-10

Austria, 112-13

Autoline, 82-83

Automation, 22-23, 27. *See also* specific systems

Automobiles (cars), 10-11, 14ff., 22-23, 27, 33-34, 40, 60, 75-89, 90-100. (*See also* Highways; specific systems); and air pollution. (*See* Air pollution); electric, 3-4, 93-95ff., 123-29; jet-propelled, 68; piggy-backing, 112-16; and zoning regulations, 36

Auto-Train, 113-14

Baltimore, Md., 78

Barges, 140

Batteries, 96-97

Bell Aerospace, 136

Bell Aerosystems, 100, 157

Bell Telephone, 90

Beltways, 78

Benson Gyrocopter, 102-103

Boeing Company, 35, 132, 133; 747, 162; SST, 165-66

Booz, Allen Applied Research, Inc., 136

Boston, Mass., 10, 13, 20, 35, 42, 78

Bouladon Integrator, 105-6

Braking, 43, 52, 64-65, 66. *See also* specific systems

British, the. *See* Great Britain and the British

Bronx River Parkway, 79

Brussels, Belgium, 39

Buffalo, N.Y., 126

Buses, 15, 27, 36, 92-93, 104, 121-23, 126; fatalities, 60; rail-bus systems, 118-21

Caesar, Julius, 77

California Urban Region, 11

Calspan Corporation (formerly Cornell Aeronautical Laboratory), 83, 123-24, 151

Cannon, Robert H., 172

Capsules, 106ff. *See also* specific systems

Carbon monoxide, 90ff.

Carr, Donald E., 95

Cars. *See* Automobiles

Central Business Districts (CBDs), 10, 14, 15, 31ff., 78, 123. *See also* specific systems

Century Expressway, 83-84

Chicago, Ill., 10, 13, 27, 33, 75-77; Congress Street Expressway, 84

182

183

184

Picture Credits

J. W. Poynter Jr. H. S. Library
1535 N. E. Grant St.
Hillsboro, Oregon 97123

187

WITHDRAWN
From
Poynter Jr. High Library